● **IN BOSTON, 1887,**

clairvoyant Lenore E. Piper so astonished skeptic William James with her intimate knowledge about his family that he stated, "I now believe her to be in possession of a power as yet unexplained."

● **IN LONDON, 1937,**

a medium performed a fraud-proof seance in which psychic researcher Dr. Harry Price was able to touch and speak with a materialized apparition. Dr. Price said of his experience, "There are no words to express what I felt—a supreme scientific interest with a feeling of absolute incredulity."

Evidence of supernatural powers linked with life after death has occurred again and again throughout man's history. Here is the book that describes how science is now investigating these phenomena and the impressive conclusions it has reached about the subject of human immortality.

Other SIGNET Mystic Books

Immortality

THE SCIENTIFIC EVIDENCE

by Alson J. Smith

A SIGNET MYSTIC BOOK

PUBLISHED BY THE NEW AMERICAN LIBRARY,
NEW YORK AND TORONTO
THE NEW ENGLISH LIBRARY LIMITED, LONDON

Books by Alson J. Smith

Faith to Live By
Brother Van
Chicago's Left Bank
Live All Your Life
Psychic Source Book
Religion and the New Psychology

SIGNET TRADEMARK REG. U.S. PAT. OFF. AND FOREIGN COUNTRIES
REGISTERED TRADEMARK—MARCA REGISTRADA
HECHO EN CHICAGO, U.S.A.

SIGNET MYSTIC BOOKS are published in the United States by The New American Library, Inc., 1301 Avenue of the Americas, New York, New York 10019, in Canada by The New American Library of Canada Limited, 295 King Street East, Toronto 2, Ontario, in the United Kingdom by The New English Library Limited, Barnard's Inn, Holborn, London, E. C. 1, England

PRINTED IN THE UNITED STATES OF AMERICA

DEDICATED
    to the memory of Leon Cushing Prince,
Professor of History at Dickinson College and
a distant cousin of the author, who started him
thinking about these things many years ago on
a green campus in a sleepy Pennsylvania town.

Contents

*May it not be that some day from this dream of
time
This chronicle of smoke, this strange and bitter
miracle of life
In which we are the moving and phantasmal
figures,
We shall awake?*

THOMAS WOLFE

EDITOR'S PREFACE

The Reverend Alson J. Smith, one of the foremost researchers linking religion with the study of psychical phenomena, died May 16, 1965, at the age of 56, in Canaan, Connecticut. When he wrote *Immortality: The Scientific Evidence*, he was obviously deeply concerned with the need to strengthen the impact of religious, and particularly Christian, thought on contemporary civilization. In this respect, he anticipated today's fermentation of ideas and practices within the Protestant and Catholic churches, as well as the profoundly provocative controversy that found expression in the recent "God is Dead" slogan.

In his Preface to the original edition of this work, the Reverend Smith stated:

Nearly two thousand years ago, the quality of its life and the universality of its instruments enabled Christianity to infuse new vigor into a decaying society. It asserted the primacy of spirit over flesh, right over wrong, life over death. Amidst falling standards it raised a new, strong standard and soon rallied about itself all that was best in the dissolving Roman Empire. At the same time it reached out to convert the barbarians from the North; Roman civilization with its law and learning was married in the Church to the savage power and moral strength of barbarism. The issue of that marriage was Western civilization.

Today we have come almost full circle. Western civilization stands where Rome stood at the beginning of the Christian era, besieged from without, full of doubt within. That the Church as an institution has social utility is unquestioned; what is open to question is how long it can retain social utility with its theological and dogmatic supports whittled away by modern science and its inner life subject to the same malaise that afflicts the outer world.

What manner of man was this Alson Jesse Smith who thought to find answers to deeply probing Ecumenical questions in the annals and experiments of psychical research and modern parapsychology? He was born on August 12, 1908, in Danbury, Connecticut. He attended Dickinson College, Carlisle, Pennsylvania, the Garrett Biblical Institute at Evanston, Illinois, and Yale University. He began his career as a social worker in Chicago, served as minister in Montana in 1933 and 1934, and later with churches in Waterbury, Meriden, and Stamford (all in Connecticut), as well as in Bayport and Brooklyn, New York.

From 1954 until his death, Alson Smith was active as an author and lecturer. Although no longer a practicing minister, religion remained of lasting interest to him, even when he researched and wrote on wordly matters. From 1945 to 1949, he was Editor of the *Social Questions Bulletin*, published by the Methodist Federation for Social Action. A listing of his books may be found elsewhere in this volume. In his Preface to the original edition, the Reverend Smith also stated:

Loving the Church for what it has meant and for what it can still mean, there have been some men and women in our day who have tried to revivify its life through an infusion from the spiritual, or psychic, side. The Church, it must be remembered, is based squarely on a psychic phenomenon—the resurrection of Jesus. Without that great, paranormal event in history there would have been no Christian Church. And buttressing that foundation are a whole series of psychic phenomena—healings, conversions, stigmata, miracles. Some who love the Church—the late Dr. Joseph Fort Newton, Dr. John Haynes Holmes, Bishop Austin Pardue, the late Fulton Oursler, Dr. Norman Vincent Peale, and others—have believed with the author that the declining power and lost authority of the Church can only be restored from the psychical side—that it is only as men, like St. Thomas of old, actually see for themselves the signs of the supernatural that they will fall to their knees in adoration of it; that only as they see the sick healed through faith not nineteen hundred years ago but before their very eyes will they believe such healing possible; that only as man's immortality is attested to by a present-day authority which they respect, will they begin to live as though in Eternity.

In other words, the lost life of the Church can only be restored through a verification, by science through experiment, of the psychic phenomena on which the Church was originally built. Men in our day are not going to turn to agglomerations of ecclesiastical power, or to glorified Crime Commissions, or to busybody Temperance Societies in their unending but increasingly desperate search for the bread of life and the meat that perishes not. They will turn, in joy and gratitude, to a Church which not only asserts the primacy of the spiritual world but demonstrates that primacy in its own corporate life.

It is time for another marriage—this time between religious experience and the scientific method. The issue of such a marriage, I believe, will be a revived Church and new hope for all mankind. Our problems are insoluble today only as we try to confront them without the resources of the spiritual world. When we find those resources and know them to be real, we do, in truth, mount up with wings as eagles; we run and are not weary; we walk and do not faint.

Only two months after the Reverend Smith's death, the ideas discussed in this volume were among the subjects of an international conference on "Religion and Parapsychology," held in June, 1965, at St. Paul de Vence, France, under the chairmanship of Canon H. L. Puxley of Toronto, Canada; among the participants were Monsignor Corrado Balducci, Jerusalem, Jordan, and Prof. S. Hugo Bergman, Hebrew University, Israel, as well as scholars in the field of Buddhism and Islam. Parapsychological phenomena have since been discussed in such Russian journals as *Science and Religion* (notably in the issues for July, 1965, and March, 1966). Dr. J. B. Rhine, whom the Reverend Smith cites in this work, has made those aspects of parapsychology that he regards as "experimental religion" a key aspect of the Foundation for Research on the Nature of Man, which he directs at Durham, North Carolina. Clearly, the ideas put forward by Alson J. Smith provide a firm foundation for contemporary practical and theoretical studies.

1

THE SPECTRAL CENSUS

THE SURVIVAL OF SOME PART OF THE HUMAN SPIRIT, OR personality, beyond the grave had been felt as an intuitive truth by men since the beginning of time. Philosophically, such survival was logical. Theology made it a tenet of religious faith. And back of the intuition, the logic, and the faith was the written and oral record of experience—of which, perhaps, Christ risen from the dead was the most dramatic illustration. The history, the folklore, the literature, the music, the art, and the religion of the race provided a rich depository of alleged overcomings of the barrier that men called death.

All this was enough for the mind of man up to and through the medieval period. He accepted the authority of religion and the logic of philosophy, which assured him that what he felt intuitively was indeed true. What happened between the thirteenth and the twentieth centuries to cause man to turn his back on religion and philosophy and question his own intuition?

The answer is: science. Modern science (which began around the middle of the sixteenth century and reached its fullest flowering in the late nineteenth and early twentieth centuries) emerged from its struggle for survival with the Church with a vast contempt for that world of the spirit of which the Church was the defender. Science was materialistic and skeptical; its method was experimental, and only what could be demonstrated experimentally in the laboratory had any meaning for it. Moreover, it was tremendously successful. It produced unheard-of wonders in its test tubes. It conquered disease and extended the life span. It caught energy

15

from the sun and water and translated it into better living. It enabled man to know the history of the material universe. So great and overwhelming were its accomplishments that, at least for Western man, it completely displaced philosophy and religion as a source of authority. The scientific *rationale* became the only one that counted. When men wanted to bestow their highest praise on something, they no longer said "it's logical," or "it's scriptural." They said "it's scientific." To say of anything that it was "unscientific" was to damn it out of hand. Even within the ranks of organized religion the scientific method which had delivered such a lethal blow to theological authority gained tacit acceptance. Mary Baker Eddy when she founded her church could think of no finer title for it than "Christian *Science*."

The authority of science, although considerably shaken today by the scientist's own alarm at what he has done recently, remains great—greater than any other authority in our world. We may say that there are many things that are outside the realm of science; that science does not conflict with philosophy and religion, etc. This may be true, but what of it? The fact remains that in our day nothing can be accepted that science does not accept, and science touches, in one way or another, every area of life and thought. As *psychology* it touches the psyche and the personality; as *medicine* it touches the body and the brain; as *chemistry* and *physics* and *biology* and all the subdivisions thereof it touches the whole physical universe.

In other words, the survival of the human personality beyond the grave will never be generally accepted—with that kind of acceptance that *means* something, that changes life—until science accepts it. This is unfortunate, perhaps, even unfair. But it is true. Even the Church will not do more than give lip-service to the idea of immortality until science sets its seal upon it.

In England, in the year 1882, a group of scholars met—classicists, philosophers, and scientists—who were interested in the question (as who isn't) of the survival of the human personality beyond death. They accepted the scientific method; they recognized the fact that the only evidence of survival which was worthwhile was evidence which would satisfy science, evidence which was acquired and analyzed according to the scientific method. They realized, moreover, that any new knowledge that was acquired would have to be continuous with the mass of knowledge already built up, and would have to grow out of that knowledge. It could not come as a "revelation" or as evidence that seemed at variance with what men already knew about the cosmos. If it did, science would throw it out. These men, imbued with respect for the scientific method, agreed that this was so, and, indeed, that it should be so.

For a long time Cambridge University in England had been the center of a considerable interest in psychic matters. As early as 1852, the Cambridge Ghost Society had been founded by Edward White Benson, who later became Archbishop of Canterbury. Bishop Lightfoot and Professor Hort, two of the leading churchmen of that day, were members of the group, as well as others from the fields of philosophy and science.

In 1882, Professor (later Sir) William Barrett, F.R.S., a physicist of impeccable scientific reputation from the Royal College of Science in Dublin, came to Cambridge to meet with some of the group there. Associating themselves with him in his interest in psychic matters were Frederic W. H. Myers, the eminent classicist at Cambridge, the philosopher Henry Sidgwick, and Dr. Edmund Gurney, a young classical scholar who also possessed a degree in medicine and who was a leading authority on the then-new technique of hypnotism. They decided to organize themselves into a group which would adhere strictly to scientific method and would investigate psychic phenomena, make studies and experiments, and otherwise endeavor to make psychical research scientifically respectable. They called the new organization The Society for Psychical Research and established headquarters in London.

They soon brought into the Society such brilliant and distinguished individuals as John Strutt (later Lord Rayleigh) and J. J. Thomson, both eminent physicists; Bateson, the biologist who was then reviving interest in the theories of Mendel; Sir William Crookes, inventor of the Crookes tube and a president of the Royal Society; Alfred Russel Wallace, who shares with Charles Darwin the credit for discovering the principle of natural selection; and many others. Many distinguished men from other lands affiliated with the London Society: Professor William James in the United States, Cesare Lombroso in Italy, Camille Flammarion in France, Albert Freiherr von Schrenck-Notzing in Germany, to name only a few. In 1885 an American Society was founded, and continues today with headquarters in New York. Affiliated with it have been men like James, Josiah Royce, Dr. Morton Prince, and L. Pearsall Smith.

One would have to look far to find names of higher professional reputation. There was nothing even remotely "fakey" about the group; nothing even very colorful. It was a body of solid, intellectually curious, respected men in science and philosophy who were out to get the truth regardless of where the truth lay.

So, for the first time since the establishment of the supreme authority of science, a group of intelligent men imbued with the scientific spirit and employing the scientific method came to grips with the great questions of life and death that science had previously designated as irrelevant (by keeping silent about them).

The first large work to which the Society for Psychical Research set itself was the collecting and analyzing of what are usually called "ghost stories"—that is, instances where apparitions or phantasms of those who are dead or dying are allegedly seen by someone still living. The group studied thousands of these "ghost stories" from all over the world and interviewed hundreds of people who claimed to have seen the apparitions. The findings were published in three great works which even today stand as the classics of the literature of psychical research. They are *Phantasms of the Living,* published in 1886, *The Census of Hallucinations,* published in 1894, and Frederic W. H. Myers' *Human Personality and Its Survival of Bodily Death,* which appeared in 1903. *Phantasms and Human Personality* contained scores of carefully chosen, rigorously documented case histories, and *Census* was an analysis of some seven thousand replies which had been received to a questionnaire which the Society sent out.

By means of statistical techniques based on the known death rate, it was possible for the Society to prove (in *Census)* that apparitions of those who were not known to be sick or in danger appeared with great frequency at or about the time of death. The Society concluded that "the number of death-coincidences in our collection is *not due to chance."* The inference was that at death something within the individual which was not bound up with the ordinary tasks of life was able to escape from the dissolving physical body and make contact briefly with those who were emotionally linked to him. This contact, thought the Society's researchers, was established telepathically—that is, a telepathic impression, a sort of cry for help, went from the subconscious mind of the dying person or the person newly dead, and was received by the subconscious mind of a living person who had been close to him and then externalized as a visual or auditory hallucination, or "ghost."

In other words, the subconscious mind of the dying person or the person recently dead was a sort of psychic television transmitter, sending a picture-signal which the subconscious receiving set of the person emotionally linked to him picked up and projected as a picture of the one at, near, or just beyond the point of death. This picture was the apparition, or "ghost." It was as weird as television itself. Also as real! And it provided *indirect* evidence of the survival of some part of the human personality for at least a short time after death.

World War I brought some rather striking corroboration of the phantasm theory that the Society for Psychical Research had arrived at as a result of *Phantasms of the Living* and *The Census of Hallucinations*. One good example from the files of the Society is the following:

The percipient was Lieutenant J. J. Larkin, of the R.A.F., and the apparition was that of one of his fellow officers, Lieutenant David M'Connel, killed in an airplane crash on December 7, 1919. Larkin reported that he spent the afternoon of December 7 reading and writing in his room at the barracks. He sat in front of the fire and was wide awake all the time. At about 3:30 P.M. he heard someone walking up the passage. "The door opened with the usual noise and clatter which David always made; I heard his 'Hello boy!' and I turned half round in my chair and saw him standing in the doorway, half in and half out of the room, holding the door knob in his hand. He was dressed in his full flying clothes but wearing his naval cap, there being nothing unusual in his appearance. . . . In reply to his 'Hello boy!' I remarked, 'Hello. Back already?' He replied, 'Yes. Got there all right, had a good trip.' . . . I was looking at him the whole time he was speaking. He said, 'Well, cheerio!' closed the door noisily and went out." Shortly after this a friend dropped in to see Larkin and Larkin told him that he had just seen and talked with Lieutenant M'Connel. (This friend sent a corroborative statement to the SPR.) Later on that day it was learned that M'Connel had been instantly killed in a flying accident which occurred at about 3:25 P.M. Mistaken identity seems to be ruled out, since the light was very good in the room where the apparition appeared. Moreover, there was no other man in the barracks at the time who in any way resembled Lieutenant M'Connel. It was also found that M'Connel was wearing his naval cap when he was killed—apparently an unusual circumstance. Agent and percipient had been "very good friends though not intimate friends in the true sense of the word."*

This was pretty convincing stuff, but it was possible to criticize it. It could be said that perhaps the fact of death was such an emotional shock that the dying person was a more powerful telepathic-transmitter than he would otherwise be and that, while the proof for telepathy was pretty convincing, it had not been proved that the human personality could survive for a *long period* after death. If the impression was received and the "ghost" seen only a few hours or even a few days after death, perhaps it was due to some sort of psychic time lag, with the impression actually having been *received* at the time of death and not welling up into consciousness and being externalized as a "ghost" until some time later. Were there any instances where a "ghost" had been seen weeks, months, or years after death?

There were. F. W. H. Myers cites a good one in *Human Personality* with the apparition being perceived two and a half months after the death, a death of which the person who saw the apparition was ignorant:

A Mrs. Clark stated that a young gentleman by the name of Akhurst had been much attached to her and had wanted to marry her. She became engaged to Mr. Clark, however, and later married him. After she had been married for about two years, Akhurst came to visit them in their home in Newcastle-on-Tyne. It appeared that at this time he was still interested in her. Akhurst then went to Yorkshire and Mrs. Clark never heard from him again. Three months passed, and her baby was born. At the end of September, 1880, very early one morning as she was feeding her baby, "I felt a cold waft of air through the room and a feeling as though someone touched my shoulder. . . . Raising my eyes to the door (which faced me) I saw Akhurst standing in his shirt and trousers looking at me, when he seemed to pass through the door. In the morning I mentioned it to my husband." Mr. Clark wrote in corroboration, "Shortly after my wife had been confined of my second daughter, about the end of September, 1880, my wife one morning informed me she had seen Akhurst about one o'clock that morning. I of course

*From a report by Mrs. Henry Sidgwick in the *Proceedings of the Society for Psychical Research* [London], Vol. XXXIII [1923], pp. 151-60.

told her it was nonsense, but she persisted, and said he appeared to her with only his trousers and a shirt on . . ."
Upon inquiry, it was learned that Akhurst had died (as a result of an overdose of chloral) on July 12, 1880. A friend said that Akhurst was found dressed only in shirt and trousers. The interval between death and apparition is thus seen to be about ten weeks.*

But in both the Larkin and Akhurst cases, the apparition was seen by only one person. An instance in which the apparition was seen at a considerable period after death by more than one person would seem more evidential. Such a case is cited in *Phantasms of the Living,* and is backed up by the affidavits of the people concerned. Here is a summary of the case in the words of Mr. Charles A. W. Lett, of the Military and Royal Naval Club, London:

December 3rd, 1885

On the 5th April 1873 my wife's father, Captain Towns, died at his residence, Cranbrook, Rose Bay, near Sidney, N.S. Wales. About six weeks after his death my wife had occasion, one evening about nine o'clock, to go to one of the bedrooms in the house. She was accompanied by a young lady, Miss Berthon, and as they entered the room—the gas was burning all the time—they were amazed to see, reflected as it were on the polished surface of the wardrobe, the image of Captain Towns. It was barely half a figure, the head, shoulders, and part of the arms only showing—in fact, it was like an ordinary medallion portrait, but life-size. The face appeared wan and pale, as it did before his death, and he wore a kind of grey flannel jacket, in which he had been accustomed to sleep. Surprised and half alarmed at what they saw, their first idea was that a portrait had been hung in the room, and that what they saw was its reflection; but there was no picture of any kind.

Whilst they were looking and wondering, my wife's sister, Miss Towns, came into the room, and before either of the others had time to speak she exclaimed, "Good Gracious! Do you see papa?" One of the housemaids happened to be passing downstairs at the moment, and she was called in, and asked if she saw anything, and her reply was, "Oh, miss! the master." Graham—Captain Towns' old body servant—was then sent for, and he also immediately exclaimed, "Oh, Lord save us! Mrs. Lett, it's the Captain!" The butler was called, and then finally Mrs. Crane, my wife's nurse, and they both said what they saw. Finally, Mrs. Towns was sent for, and, seeing the apparition, she advanced towards it with her arm

*London: Longmans, Green & Co., 1903, Vol. II, p. 371.

extended as if to touch it, and as she passed her hand over the panel of the wardrobe the figure gradually faded away, and never again appeared, though the room was regularly occupied for a long time after.*

There were also a number of cases in which the ghost or apparition appeared in a form which had characterized it at a certain period of life in which it was unknown or out of touch with the person to whom it later appeared. For instance, perhaps the "ghost" was seen wearing a beard, which would appear strange to a friend who had not known him during that period of life in which he had worn a beard. These cases were particularly convincing because if the whole thing was *originating* in some way in the mind of the person who saw the apparition, he would not be likely to see it in any other form except that which had been familiar to him when the ghost was alive. To have apparitions appear in forms different from what the persons who saw them had been familiar with in life, and then to have this unknown difference (that the deceased actually *had* worn a beard when a young man, etc.) later verified, greatly buttresses the case for believing that these apparitions actually did represent some activity of the human personality beyond the grave. A good illustration of this type of case is reported in Myers' *Human Personality*, Vol. II, pp. 27-30. In this often-quoted case, a commercial traveler saw his sister's apparition with a red scratch on its cheek. When the young man mentioned his experience to his mother, she explained that she had accidentaly made just such a scratch on her daughter's cheek while preparing the body for burial. She had carefully obliterated it with powder and had never told a living soul about the incident. It is interesting to note that the girl had been dead for nine years when her apparition was perceived.

Another class of cases which seemed to point directly toward the survival of the human personality after death was that in which the apparition was of someone who was unknown to the person who saw it, and had to be identified later. These cases were important, because they completely ruled out the criticism that perhaps the whole thing (the seeing of the apparitions) was merely a matter of telepathy between people who were linked emotionally. (We all know how people who are very close emotionally—husband and

*London: Trubner & Co., 1886, Vol. II, p. 213.

wife, lovers, brothers and sisters, etc.—tend to know what is in each other's mind, so that they utter the same sentence at the same time, etc.) But if the person who sees the apparition had never known the ghost in life and the latter is only identified later by someone else, then the criticism falls down. One such instance analyzed by the Society for Psychical Research is the following:

In January or February of 1885, the percipient, Mr. Husbands, was sleeping in a hotel in Madeira. It was a bright moonlight night; his windows were open and the blinds up. "I felt some one was in my room," Mr. Husbands wrote. "On opening my eyes I saw a young fellow about 25, dressed in flannels, standing at the side of my bed and pointing with the first finger of his right hand to the place I was lying. I lay for some seconds to convince myself of some one being really there. I then sat up and looked at him. I saw his features so plainly that I recognized them in a photograph which was shown me some days after. . . . As I was going to spring out of my bed he slowly vanished through the door, which was shut, keeping his eyes upon me all the time." Another resident in the hotel, Miss Falkner, wrote: "The figure that Mr. Husbands saw while in Madeira was that of a young fellow who died unexpectedly months previously (in January, 1884), in the room which Mr. Husbands was occupying. Curiously enough, Mr. H. had never heard of him or his death. He told me the story the morning after he had seen the figure, and I recognized the young fellow from the description." Mr. Husbands also correctly described a costume, a cricket or tennis suit, which the dead man often wore."*

One of the most intriguing court cases on record is one involving the activity of an apparition, and it is particularly significant in that it shows *initiative* on the part of the deceased. It is called "The Chaffin Will Case," and is the only instance in modern legal history in which a ghost succeeded in changing a court decision.

James L. Chaffin was a well-to-do, rather eccentric farmer who lived in Davie County, North Carolina. He married and had four sons—John, James, Marshall, and Abner, in order of age. Of these, Marshall was his favorite, although he loved all of his children and tried to treat them impartially.

However, when he was along in years, he was gently urged by the family to make his will, and when he did so (on No-

*From *Proceedings of the Society for Psychical Research* [London], Vol. V [1888], pp. 415-16.

vember 16, 1905) he executed a document which left no
doubt in anyone's mind that Marshall was his special pride
and joy. In a will which was duly attested by two witnesses
and which he made no effort to keep secret, he appointed
Marshall sole executor of his estate and bequeathed the family farm and everything else to him. His wife and three other
sons were left completely out in the cold. The disinherited
spouse and children were understandably miffed, but put the
whole thing down to the old man's eccentricity. Life went on
for the Chaffins without too much friction in spite of the unfair will.

On September 7, 1921, the elder Chaffin finally shuffled off
this mortal coil after a fall downstairs, and on September 24
Marshall Chaffin obtained probate of the will. The mother
and three other brothers did not contest, knowing that it was
a valid document. The will was duly probated and entered in
the court records as "closed," and the property was turned
over to Marshall.

Four years passed—quietly, uneventfully. Four years of
farm work, family picnics, churchgoing, and an occasional
movie on Saturday night at the county seat for the Chaffin
boys, their wives and children, and their aged mother. The
property now belonged to Marshall, but otherwise things
went on as before and whatever irritation the disinherited had
felt gradually disappeared.

Then, one night in early June, 1925, James Chaffin had a
dream so vivid and unearthly that he awoke bathed in sweat.
He had been dreaming a lot for several weeks previously, and
mostly about his father. But on this particular night, as he
dozed in that intermediate state between sleeping and waking
that we all sometimes experience, his father suddenly appeared at his bedside. The old man was dressed as he had
been in life, and he wore the long black overcoat which had
been his trade-mark in Davie County for at least ten winters.
In his dream, James saw his father pull open the overcoat
and point to an inside pocket. Again and again he pointed to
the pocket. Abruptly the vision faded, and James Chaffin
awoke, sweating and trembling.

After breakfast that morning, James went over to the old
farmhouse where his mother was still living. He felt a bit
foolish, but the dream had been so vivid that he knew he
would have no peace until he had found the old overcoat and
looked into the inside pocket.

The elder Mrs. Chaffin remembered the coat very clearly. Yes, that black overcoat of Pa's—seems to me I gave that to John.

John Chaffin, the oldest of the brothers, lived in Yadkin County, about twenty miles away. The following Monday, James drove up to see him. John was out, but his wife remembered the coat. It was hanging upstairs in a closet, and had been ever since Mrs. Chaffin, Sr., had given it to John. He had worn it only once or twice. It was too big.

Together John Chaffin's wife and James Chaffin took the old black coat down from its hanger and laid it on the bed. Nervously, James drew it open and ran his fingers along the inside pocket. It was sewn shut! He cut the stitches and reached inside. His fingers closed around a tiny roll of yellow paper tied with a string. He untied the string, opened the paper, and read these words in his father's handwriting:

"Read the 27th Chapter of Genesis in my daddy's old Bible."

James's grandfather, Nathan S. Chaffin, had been a clergyman. His Bible was a fragile, worn affair, one of the most treasured Chaffin family heirlooms, and it was kept in a top bureau drawer in an upstairs bedroom of the old Chaffin farmhouse in Davie County. James, thoroughly excited by now, immediately drove back to the old farm. But before he left, he and John's wife looked up the 27th chapter of Genesis in the Bible at John's home. It told the story of how the younger brother, Jacob, supplanted the other brother, Esau, and won his birthright and his father's blessing.

James now decided that he should not go any farther without witnesses. He got in touch with a neighbor, Mr. Thomas Blackwelder, and induced Mr. Blackwelder and the latter's daughter to accompany him and his own daughter to his mother's house. (Mr. Blackwelder later made an affidavit on everything that happened from this point on.)

Solemnly James Chaffin and his three witnesses followed the elder Mrs. Chaffin upstairs to the bedroom where the Bible was kept. Mrs. Chaffin opened the drawer and James lifted out the old book—which immediately fell in three pieces to the floor. James picked up two of the pieces and Mr. Blackwelder one. The one which Mr. Blackwelder retrieved was the one containing the Book of Genesis. At the 27th chapter two leaves had been folded over so as to form a pocket, and in this pocket was found a paper on which was written, in the elder Chaffin's handwriting:

After reading the 27th Chapter of Genesis, I, James L. Chaffin, do make my last will and testament, and here it is. I want, after giving my body a decent burial, my little property to be equally divided between my four children, if they are living at my death, both personal and real estate divided equal, if not living with share going to their children. And if she is living, you all must take care of your mammy. Now this is my last will and testament. Witness my hand and seal.

James L. Chaffin
This January 16, 1919

Although this second will was unattested, it was legal in North Carolina if it could be proved that the handwriting was that of the elder Chaffin. It obviously was; nobody ever questioned it. James thereupon submitted the second will to the court for probation with a plea to set aside the first will.

Marshall had since died, so his young son was made a defendant in the suit to set aside the first will and prove the second. Marshall's widow agreed to appear in court as her son's guardian *ad litem* and next friend.

The case, however, was never tried. Just before it was scheduled to be tried, Marshall Chaffin's widow was shown the second will and immediately agreed that it was in the elder Chaffin's handwriting and therefore valid. The court thereupon ordered the first will canceled and the second will was probated.

The Chaffin Will Case created quite a furor in Davie County. Skeptics accused James of forging the second will, but handwriting experts vindicated him. Psychologists announced that he had probably heard his father speak of a second will at some time, and had carried the information in his subconscious mind all the while. But all members of the Chaffin family insisted that the old man had never spoken of a second will. Some researchers talked learnedly of "delayed telepathy."

However, all attempts to explain the case in normal terms failed, and it stands in the record as the only instance in modern times in which a dream has been directly responsible for a court ruling.

A final category of apparition-appearances is that which the psychical researchers have called "Peak in Darien" cases (From Keats's "On First Looking into Chapman's Homer"). In these cases there appears to be spontaneous activity on the part of *two* entities—one dead, and the other still living but near death. The chief feature of these cases is the perception

by the dying person of a phantasm of a dead person who is
not known by the dying person to be dead at all. Sir William
Barrett, in his book *The Death-Bed Visions,* gives several illustrations of this type. One of them concerns a girl dying of
tuberculosis:

> She had lain for some days in a prostrate condition taking
> no notice of anything, when she opened her eyes, and . . .
> said "Susan—and Jane—and Ellen," as if recognizing the pres-
> ence of her three sisters, who had previously died of the
> same disease. Then . . . she continued, "and Edward
> too!"—naming a brother then supposed to be alive and well
> in India—as if surprised at seeing him in the company. She
> said no more and sank shortly afterwards. In the course of
> the post, letters came from India announcing the death of
> Edward, from an accident a week or two previous to the
> death of his sister . . .*

What can be said of these "phantasm" cases? Are they evidences of the survival of some part of the human personality,
the human intelligence, beyond the experience that we call
death?

It would seem so. At least, the eminent scientists, psychologists, and scholars who analyzed the phantasms and hallucinations for the Society for Psychical Research came to the conclusion that these so-called ghosts did indeed represent a genuine invasion by the deceased—an actual breaking through
by conscious entities on the other side of the grave, into the
experience, the "life-space" of those still living. And no convincing alternative explanation was ever offered.

This was not, to be sure, official Science affirming that here
for the first time was scientifically respectable evidence that
there is conscious, individual, active life beyond the arbitrary
boundary we call death. But it was a group of individual
scientists (among others) of the highest integrity affirming it
as their belief that here was convincing evidence, gathered
and analyzed by the scientific method, that Job's ancient
question: "If a man die, shall he live again?" could be
answered with a quiet but firm yes.

*London: Methuen & Co. Ltd., 1928.

2

TRANCE TESTIMONY

THROUGHOUT HISTORY WE FIND INDIVIDUALS WHO HAVE claimed to possess the strange gift of mediumship—the capacity for acting as intermediary between the physical world and the spiritual world, the living and the dead. The Delphic Oracle—the Pythoness—was a medium; so were the "soothsayers and Chaldeans" of the Bible. So, in a sense, were the "witches" who were burned at Salem. Whole religious sects have been based on the idea of some sort of a nexus between those in the flesh and those in the spirit—the carnate and the discarnate. Modern Spiritualism, with its minister-mediums, is more than a cult; it is a world-wide church with hundreds of thousands of members.

That mediumship is a talent that lends itself easily to fraud is obvious. The opportunities for exploiting the credulous and the bereaved are innumerable. The tricks of the trade are so perfected that almost any clever charlatan can purchase the right props, set himself up as a medium, and produce phenomena that will fool all but the most astute observers.

The Society for Psychical Research, realizing from the beginning that it was venturing on ground that was booby-trapped with all manner of nonsense, early became the mortal foe of the phony medium. Both the English and the American Societies systematically exposed many a faker, and in doing so often incurred the wrath of some estimable people who had faith in the charlatan. In England, Sir Arthur Conan Doyle and William Crookes both clashed with the SPR when its investigations proved the fraudulence of their favorite mediums. As I write these words, I have before me a pamphlet which just arrived in the mail from Boston. It is put out by a Spiritualist group there and denounces "psychical research" as a science which is diabolically determined to destroy Spiritualism.

Yet, digging stubbornly in the haystack of nonsense and fakery for a slender needle of truth, the psychical researchers and the parapsychologists have uncovered some mediums who have stood every test that the men of science, using the scientific method, could devise. Here and there they found a medium of unquestioned integrity, producing phenomena that went far to prove what the researchers themselves called the "survival hypothesis." There were ten, perhaps a hundred, fakers for every honest medium, but, as William James once observed, it takes only one white crow to prove that not all crows are black.

For William James, professor of psychology at Harvard and founder of the Pragmatic School, the one white crow that went far to prove that survival was a fact was the woman who was probably the greatest medium America has yet produced—Mrs. Leonore E. Piper, of Boston.

Professor James first heard of Mrs. Piper in 1885. She had been practicing mediumship for only a year, having discovered her own mediumistic faculties when she consulted another medium about a medical problem. A friend who knew Mrs. Piper had spoken to the mother of Dr. James's wife about her, and this lady, whose name was Gibbens, paid a visit to Mrs. Piper. She had never visited a medium before, and returned home full of stories of how Mrs. Piper had told her facts about the family, knowledge of which she could not have obtained normally. Dr. James tried to disillusion her, explaining how mediums could trick people, etc., but he was curious enough to visit Mrs. Piper subsequently himself. At his first sitting with her, she showed so much knowledge of the James family affairs, deceased relatives, etc., that the professor was taken aback. He visited her several times and sent a number of other people to her, all of whom later reported back to him. He finally stated: "I am persuaded of the medium's honesty, and of the genuineness of her trance; and although at first disposed to think that the 'hits' she made were either lucky coincidences, or the result of knowledge on her part of whom the sitter was and of his or her family affairs, I now believe her to be in possession of a power as yet unexplained."

In 1887, Professor James introduced Mrs. Piper to Dr. Richard Hodgson, who had just come over from England to act as research officer for the American Society for Psychical Research. From that time on Mrs. Piper was investigated almost constantly by both the American and British Societies for Psychical Research.

In 1889 Mrs. Piper went to England, where she was investigated intensively by the researchers of the British Society, including Sir Oliver Lodge, Professor Walter Leaf, Professor Henry Sidgwick, and F. W. H. Myers. They took every precaution against fraud, and yet Mrs. Piper almost immediately produced strikingly accurate phenomena. At a sitting with Sir Oliver Lodge, she established contact (through a control called Dr. Phinuit, supposed to be the spirit of a deceased French physician) with Mrs. Lodge's deceased father, although she at first wrongly identified him as "Uncle William." Later she correctly identified him as Alexander Marshall and stated that he had had an illness and had died with it. He had tried to speak to Mary, his wife, and had stretched out his hand to her. However, he couldn't reach her, and fell, and died. She went on to state that he had trouble with his right leg when alive, and that the trouble was due to a fall, that it was below the knee, and that it kept him in a good deal of pain. She also said that Mr. Marshall had had a great deal of trouble with his teeth, and had traveled a lot and wore a uniform with big, bright buttons on it.

All of these statements turned out to be correct. Mr. Marshall had been a captain in the merchant service and of course had traveled a great deal in the course of his work. Also, he did wear a uniform with bright buttons on it. Once he had fallen down a hole and broken his right leg just below the knee. He also suffered from toothache, and the facts attending his death were correct. Later she told the Lodges a number of other accurate facts about various members of their family.

Much later, in 1915—on August 8 to be exact—Mrs. Piper, in Boston, received a trance message that "a blow was about to fall" on her friends, the Lodges, in England. She immediately notified Sir Oliver, and he received her notification early in September. A few days later, the Lodges' son, Raymond, was killed at the front in France, the War Office notifying the Lodges on September 17.

Was Mrs. Piper faking all this? In some way did she obtain prior information about the Lodges, the Jameses, and other people with whom she "sat," so that she could then amaze them with her allegedly supernormal knowledge of their affairs? It is difficult to believe this. Mrs. Piper was a woman against whom no imputation of fraud was ever brought. It would not be easy to deceive men of intelligence such as James, Lodge, and Hodgson. Even though they knew and liked Mrs. Piper, they nevertheless took every precaution against deceit, for as psychologists they knew that there are people who are consciously honest but *subliminally fraudulent*. Hodgson, indeed, had Mrs. Piper shadowed by private detectives during the time that he was investigating her mediumship. At first he was extremely skeptical, but he finally concluded that:

> It may be that further experiment in the lines of investigation before us may lead me to change my view; but at the present time I cannot profess to have any doubt but that the chief "communicators" are veritably the personalities that they claim to be, that they have survived the change we call death, and that they have directly communicated with us whom we call living, through Mrs. Piper's entranced organism.*

Mrs. Piper was the best known and certainly the most rigidly tested medium in the United States. There were a few others whose honesty stood every test. One of these was Mrs. Minnie Soule, also of Boston, who is best known for her work in what is known in the annals of psychical research as the "Mother of Doris" Case.†

One of Mrs. Soule's alleged spirit controls was the aforementioned Dr. Richard Hodgson, who had died suddenly in Boston soon after his investigation of Mrs. Piper. In addition to his work with Mrs. Piper, Hodgson had also cooperated with Dr. Morton Prince of Tufts Medical School in curing a very celebrated case of multiple personality known in the research of abnormal psychology as the Beauchamp Case (about which more later).

At this time the president of the American Society for Psychical Research was Dr. James Hyslop of Columbia University. Dr. Hyslop had been investigating Mrs. Soule, and had devised a method of conducting a séance with her in which the sitter, or subject, did not enter the room until after the medium was in the trance state, sat directly *behind* the

Proceedings of the Society for Psychical Research [London], Vol. XIII [1897], pp. 405-06.
†For a full account see *Proceedings of the American Society for Psychical Research* [New York], Vol. XVI [1923].

medium so that he or she could not be seen by the medium at any time, and departed before the medium came out of the trance. Moreover, Dr. Hyslop would select the sitters without consulting Mrs. Soule. Any evidence obtained under such circumstances would seem to be quite valid.

Now—Dr. Hyslop wished to test the Hodgson control. Was this really the spirit of Dr. Richard Hodgson? If so, "Hodgson" would be familiar with the Beauchamp Case. If the subject of a similar case of multiple personality could be introduced into a séance with Mrs. Soule, unknown to her, then if "Hodgson" was really the Hodgson who had worked with Dr. Morton Prince on the Beauchamp Case, he would recognize the similarity between the two cases. If he did show some awareness of the connection between the two cases, that would be pretty good proof that he was indeed the spirit of Dr. Richard Hodgson.

This was an ingenious scheme for testing both Mrs. Soule and "Hodgson." As the subject, or sitter, Dr. Hyslop obtained a girl by the name of Doris Fischer, who five months previously had been cured of a case of multiple personality very like the Beauchamp Case. At the time Mrs. Soule had never heard of Doris Fischer. Mrs. Soule lived in Boston and Doris in California. Nothing had appeared in the papers about the case. During the sittings, Doris entered the room only after Mrs. Soule was entranced, sat behind her, and left before she came out of the trance state.

Bearing in mind all these precautions, the fact that the "spirit" most in evidence during the sittings was that of Doris Fischer's long-dead *mother* is truly remarkable. The "mother" described the childhood of Doris very minutely, indicating the source of Doris' split personality to have been in an unpleasant childhood incident in which her father, coming home drunk, had thrown her violently to the floor. The information given by the "mother" fitted in perfectly with the doctor's reconstruction and diagnosis of the case.

The mother of Doris was not wanted by Dr. Hyslop, however. He was after "Hodgson," and finally one day "Hodgson" appeared. Dr. Hyslop himself was in the room with the sitter (Doris Fischer) and the medium (Mrs. Soule), and the following conversation took place between Dr. Hyslop and "Hodgson" (through the entranced Mrs. Soule, of course):

HODGSON. I am much interested in the way this case is going on and do not think I can add much.

DR. HYSLOP. Can you compare it with any you know?

HODGSON. Yes, and have several times thought that I would interpolate a message that you might see that I recognized the similarity of the case with one in particular that caused me some concern at times and some hope at others, but this is better organized than that was. I mean that there seems to be a definite purpose and a continuity of knowledge that the other case displayed spasmodically. You will, I think, know what I mean by that.

DR. HYSLOP. Yes, I think so.

HODGSON. I will do what I can on this side to help on this case, for I believe it as important as any M.P. ever had.

DR. HYSLOP. What does "M.P." mean?

HODGSON. Morton Prince.

DR. HYSLOP. Good.

HODGSON. You see what I am after?

DR. HYSLOP. Exactly what I wanted.

HODGSON. The Beauchamp Case, and I am trying to make some clear headway out of this one more than I did out of that.

This case is one of the most evidential on record. Fraud seems to be ruled out by the elaborate precautions taken as well as by Mrs. Soule's reputation for honesty. "Hodgson's" technical knowledge of both the Beauchamp Case and the Fischer Case and his immediate connection of the two seems to rule out subliminal fraudulence on the part of Mrs. Soule, for his knowledge was far beyond hers in her normal state. It also seems to rule out the possibility that (as is alleged of many mediums) the "spirit control" (Hodgson in this case) is merely a split-off part of the medium's own personality.

One of the most industrious and best-known psychical researchers of recent years was the late Dr. Harry Price, of the University of London. Dr. Price probably exposed more fraudulent mediums than any other one man. He set up an ingenious laboratory at London complete with infra-red lights and other paraphernalia designed to trap the dishonest practitioner of the occult arts, and as the BBC's expert on psychic phenomena he broadcast from "haunted" houses and improvised various experiments which could be conducted over the air. In the middle 1930's, before the true nature of the Hitler government in Germany became clear, he accepted an invitation to establish a laboratory of parapsychology at the University of Bonn, but dropped the project before it was carried through. Price was certainly not a man to be taken in by fraud, no matter how ingenious it might be. He had written a

book exposing the tricks of the dishonest medium and was
the author of a bill to regulate the practice of mediumship
which contained the most severe penalties for fraud. His experience with "Rosalie," therefore, deserves to be taken seriously. Here it is:

On the morning of Wednesday, December 8, 1937, Dr.
Price received a telephone call from a lady, obviously well-
educated, who told him that she had heard a broadcast on
haunted houses which he had made, and inviting him to a
séance at her house. At the séance, she said, a "little girl
spirit" named Rosalie would materialize. Would he not like
to come and "test" Rosalie? He would be allowed full control
of the room and the sitters, could search the house, seal all
external windows and doors, move the furniture around,
sprinkle powdered starch around the doors and windows, put
electrical contacts anywhere he wished, search everybody and
anything. Only, once the séance had started, he was to remain passive, since the mother of Rosalie would be present
and they did not want to do anything that would frighten the
little girl and prevent her from materializing on subsequent
occasions.

Dr. Price accepted the invitation, and a week later made
the trip from London to the home of the lady who had called.
The house was in a prosperous suburb; it was a typical large
mid-Victorian, double-fronted detached suburban residence.*
Dr. Price was admitted by the maid, and was greeted by his
hosts, Mr. and Mrs. X, and their daughter, a girl of seven-
teen. They had a light supper, and during the course of the
meal, Mr. and Mrs. X told Dr. Price the story of Rosalie.

Mr. X was in business in London; he and his wife were
charming, affable, and intelligent people, not Spiritualists, but
interested in a mild way in psychical research. They had a
friend named Madame Z, whom Mrs. X had met at a church
bazaar. Madame Z was French; she had been a nurse and
had married an English officer at the beginning of World
War I. Her husband had been killed in 1916, leaving her with
a baby, Rosalie. Rosalie died of diphtheria in 1921, when she
was six.

Madame Z had moved to England after her marriage, and
was living near the Xs, in two furnished rooms. In the spring
of 1925 or thereabouts, Madame Z was awakened during the

*For a complete description of the house and a more detailed account
of this case, see Price's book *Fifty Years of Psychical Research* [New
York: Longmans, Green & Co., 1939].

night by the sound of her dead child's voice crying "Mother." This happened several times, and Madame Z began to lie awake nights, waiting for the voice! Gradually, she began to see the dim outline of Rosalie's figure and to hear her walking softly about the room. Finally one night she held out her hand toward the shadow and her hand was grasped by that of her child.

When she told Mr. and Mrs. X about this they were skeptical, but suggested that regular séances be held in their home (Madame Z's rooms were small and unsuited for such an experience) in order to encourage Rosalie. They would have in a few members of the family, dim the lights, and sit in a circle. There was no mediumistic hocus-pocus at all. For six months, nothing happened, although Rosalie continued to visit her mother at night. One night in the late spring of 1929, however, Rosalie did materialize at the séance and from then on appeared regularly. Gradually a little light was introduced by means of hand mirrors covered with luminous paint. Finally Rosalie began to speak, answering simple questions in monosyllables.

Such was the background. After supper, Madame Z arrived; she was a pleasant French lady of about fifty. A bank clerk by the name of Jim, a friend of the Xs' daughter, completed the circle of sitters.

Accompanied by Mr. X and Jim, Dr. Price made a complete tour of the house. He had brought with him the tools of the fake-medium hunter's trade—a gimlet, screw-eyes, white tape, adhesive surgical tape, a bag of powdered starch, and a flashlight. He sealed every door and window in the house with the tape and screw-eyes, tying the tape in three knots and initialling it. The cook and maid (who didn't know what took place at the séance anyway) were instructed not to answer any knock or ring.

The séance was to be held in the drawing room, and after the sitters were assembled therein, Dr. Price had all the excess furniture removed and every entrance sealed. He examined minutely the floors, the ceiling, the walls, and the fireplace, and sprinkled the powdered starch in the hall outside the door. The fireplace was effectively sealed by placing a sheet of the evening newspaper on the top bar of the lower grate and sprinkling it with starch. It was impossible for anyone to enter or leave the room without leaving a trace and the examination proved conclusively that no one was hidden in the room. Every drawer was emptied, even the settee was

dismantled and its pillows thoroughly prodded. The clothes of
the sitters were also inspected. Fraud was excluded as thoroughly as it is humanly possible to do so.

At exactly 9:10 P.M. the séance began. Dr. Price sat between Mrs. X (on his right) and Madame Z (on his left).
Next to the latter was Miss X, then Jim, and finally Mr. X.
Madame Z, Miss X, Jim and Dr. Price had the mirrors
(small hand affairs) which were covered with luminous paint.
The group chatted quietly in the darkness for a few moments. Then Mr. X groped his way to the radio and turned
on some soft music from a foreign station; after about five
minutes he turned it off again. Silence for a while, and just as
Dr. Price had concluded that it was all much ado about nothing, he heard Madame Z whisper softly, "Rosalie!" She and
Mrs. X whispered the name on and off for about twenty minutes. Miss X was sobbing quietly.

A few minutes after ten, Madame Z gave a choking sob

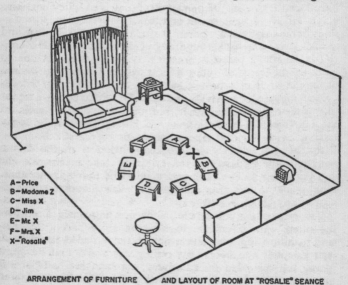

A—Price
B—Madame Z
C—Miss X
D—Jim
E—Mr. X
F—Mrs. X
X—"Rosalie"

ARRANGEMENT OF FURNITURE   AND LAYOUT OF ROOM AT "ROSALIE" SEANCE

and said, "My darling." At the same time Dr. Price realized
that there was something near him; he could not see or hear
anything but there was a sense of *presence* and an odd, rather
pleasant odor. Dr. Price slowly stretched out his hand and to

his utter amazement it came into contact with the nude figure of a little girl. The flesh felt warm, but not as warm as human flesh. He passed his hand over her chest, back, legs, and feet, and felt her long soft hair which fell shoulder length.

"There are no words," said Dr. Price, "to express how I felt—a supreme scientific interest with a feeling of absolute incredulity, would best describe my reactions." He asked permission to examine the little form. It was certainly that of a little girl about three feet seven inches tall. He felt her pulse and estimated it about 90. He put his ear to her chest and could hear her heart. With the help of the luminous mirrors, he could see that this was indubitably a beautiful child of perhaps six years. He asked her several questions, to which she gave no reply. Then he said "Do you love your mummy?" "Yes," Rosalie lisped softly.

In fifteen minutes, Rosalie was gone. Dr. Price immediately began an examination of the premises. Every seal was intact, the starch powder was undisturbed.

Dr. Price went to his room at the Royal Societies Club and there wrote a complete report of the Rosalie Case. His conclusion was that it was "amazing"—and he was not one to use that word lightly. Had it taken place in his own laboratory, he said, he would not hesitate to proclaim to an incredulous world that survival was proved! He wanted to repeat the séance in the laboratory, but Madame Z was convinced that the laboratory conditions would frighten Rosalie away and the experiment was never made.

Some friends of mine who have written in this field lean heavily on their own personal experiences to illustrate the quality of evidence that may be obtained through mediums. Nothing, of course, has quite the emotional impact of a personal experience, and nothing is quite so convincing to an individual as something that he, himself, experienced. Such personal illustrations are also highly readable, and the combination constitutes a temptation almost too great to be resisted. If I have not emphasized my own personal experience here, it is not because I have not had any, but because I believe it is difficult, if not impossible, to be scientifically objective about one's own experiences. As previously indicated, it is only as evidence that is scientifically acceptable is adduced that a study like this takes on intellectual respectability, and only if it is intellectually and scientifically acceptable will it have any weight at all in the long run. That is why I have preferred to talk about people like Mrs. Piper, Mrs. Soule, and Dr. Harry Price, rather than about myself or my friends. The experiences of these individuals may actually be no more evidential than my own, or those of my friends, but they have been rigorously examined and evaluated by trained investigators, and thus bear a stamp of scientific approval that our experiences do not have.

However, suspect as they may be as evidence, personal experiences do connect the writer in an integral way with his subject, and, if not overdone and overvalued, and if no claim for absolute accuracy of memory is made, they can add a good deal of interest to a book like this.

My own interest in psychical research goes back to my undergraduate days, but it was not until about five years ago, when I was fifteen years out of college, that that interest was much more than cursory and critical. Then, through circumstances that I will recount later, two things happened: I read Dr. J. B. Rhine's *New Frontiers of the Mind* and *The Reach of the Mind*, and I had a personal experience that sharply increased my interest in the field.

At this time I had been working closely with the Research Council on Problems of Alcohol, and I was in a large midwestern city, where I was to give an address on the subject the following day. I was whiling away some time in the lobby of my hotel when I noticed an announcement on the bulletin board of a lecture by a Hindu swami being given that evening. Since the lecture was open to the public and I had nothing better to do, I dropped in.

The meeting was fairly well attended by a well-dressed crowd made up predominantly of elderly to middle-aged women. The swami, dressed in a plain business suit but with a white turban wound tightly about his head, was suitably dark and mysterious looking, and it seemed obvious that some elaborate tomfoolery was about to be perpetrated on these naïve women as a means of separating them from as much cold cash as possible. In this frame of mind I lolled casually in an aisle seat in the last row, where I could make a quick and quiet exit if I so desired.

The swami was a member of the Ramakrishna cult, and he began with some explanatory remarks about Vedanta which, in spite of myself, I found quite absorbing. Then he read a number of poems, first in Bengali or a similar Hindu dialect and then in English, and I found that I was slowly being drawn into the mood of the meeting—relaxed, and yet somehow intensely aware. It was a surprising and restful experience.

Finally the swami announced that he was a mental medium, and would endeavor to make contact with "friends" who were "on the other side." Even in the pleasantly euphoric mood induced by his reading of the poems, I could not help but think: Ah-hah, now comes the nonsense.

He closed his eyes and rested his head gently upon one hand, his forefinger barely touching the caste-mark on his forehead. He stayed that way for perhaps a minute and a half, then his hand fell listlessly to the table and his eyes slowly opened. He looked straight out, unblinking; he was either in a self-induced trance or was faking one. When he spoke it was in a high, not-very-pleasant voice quite different from the one in which he had read the poems.

"There is a person named Eng here—is it Engberg?—no, it is Engstrom—Engstrom—a Mrs. Helen Engstrom?"

A gray-haired, stylishly dressed, sixtyish woman three seats away from me in the back row gasped. "Yes" she said, almost inaudibly. "Ellen—not Helen."

"Ellen Engstrom," said the swami. "Ellen, I have someone who claims to be your late husband, Carl—no, Charles. He wishes to say that he is well and happy—that he sees Freda often—that you must not spend so much time mourning him—that you will join him in a few years."

The woman began to sob quietly. "Oh, Charlie!" she said. She spoke to the woman next to her. "Freda was my sister. She died three months ago."

The swami went on. "Charles wishes to identify himself. He asks you to remember the book you enjoyed so much that summer at the lake—the boat book."

"I remember," said Mrs. Engstrom. "It was *Three Men in a Boat.* We laughed so over it. We were at Lake Bomoseen. It was six years ago." The woman was alternately smiling and crying.

The swami was silent for a while. Then he began again, groping for another name, making the connection with a person in the audience, delivering the "message" and the identification.

It was an amazing and moving performance. I thought to myself, Good heavens, what a clever charlatan! Were "Mrs. Engstrom" and the others confederates of his? Or had he known they were going to be present and done some research on them? I resolved to find out at the end of the meeting.

But before the end of the meeting, something happened which seemed to make such inquiry academic. The swami said: "Is there a person here with the first name of Ale-son?"

This was the most unlikely first name in the world. There were only six other men present besides myself, and none of them gave any sign of recognizing the name. Now "Ale-son" is the old Anglo-Saxon spelling of my first name, so I said as matter-of-factly as possible: "Could that be 'Alson'?"

He was quiet for a moment. Then he said, "It is 'Alson.' And the last name—Schmidt?"

"Smith," I said.

Now my speech in town, scheduled for the following night in this same hotel, was practically a secret. There had been no publicity about it. Of course, perhaps the swami had read the hotel register, but he would have had to work fast; I had not been registered for more than an hour.

He went on: "I have a middle name. It is Jesse."

That wasn't on the hotel register. I said nothing.

The swami started again: "It is your father. Jeff—no, Giff—Gifford. And the middle name—also 'Ale-son.' "

My father's name was Gifford Alson.

The swami said: "He died when you were quite young. [I was ten.] He says he has been very near you all these years. He is so glad you named one of your children 'Ale-son.' [My second child is named Philip Alson.] He says your mother is here and well. [My mother died in 1932.]"

He continued: "He identifies himself by the cigar in the shutter. He knows you will remember that."

My mother had refused to let my father smoke cigars in the house, so he had always pinched them out and stuck them in the blinds over the porch window, where he could retrieve them on leaving the house.

The meeting ended; I went up to my room. I should have talked to the swami (I didn't even make note of his name); I should have checked with the others who had received "messages" to make sure they were not colleagues of the swami's. All I can say is that I was too overwhelmed by the whole thing to have presence of mind enough to do these things. Later I confided the story of this experience to others; their only comment was that I must have been taking a more than rhetorical interest in the subject of my own speech (alcohol).

Now let me cite the experience of a good friend of mine, Dr. Amos Horlacher. Dr. Horlacher is now dean of men at my own college, Dickinson, in Pennsylvania. At the time this incident took place, he was a clergyman in Brooklyn. I cite it, not as evidence in the scientific sense, but as an example of the kind of thing that happens to so many of us and that brings us the vague feeling that "there is something to this business," even though we never go on and find out just what, if anything, there is to it. Here it is in Dr. Horlacher's own words:

The year is in the late thirties, I would say about 1938. I had read in the paper that there was to be a conference of people interested in psychic research in New York City. The time was about May of that year. I did not know that I would attend this meeting until a few hours before, and I knew no one at the meeting. It was held, as I recall, in the Hotel Roosevelt. I arrived late and took a seat somewhat in the rear of a large ballroom. During the course of that evening a number of people were told many things which seemed, from their testimony, remarkable to them. I distinctly recall that there was one medium by the name of [Arthur] Ford who was a clairaudient medium. During the course of that evening I let my mind concentrate on a young man whose name was Arthur J. Beyports. He had been a very close friend of mine at Williamsport-Dickinson Seminary from the years 1920-23. In the course of the years after I had received my degree from Union Theological Seminary, I had married him to his wife. Some years later he was the victim of an accident whereby he fell, his head struck a sharp stone, and he was almost instantly killed. In 1938 he had been dead several years, I would say about five or six years. My reason for concentrating upon him was because he was the one person whom I had known very well who had died and from whom, should there by any reality in this business, I felt I might get some communication. The evening wore on and no one on the platform seemed to take any cognizance of me because I was one of several hundred people. The chairman was about to bring the meeting to a close when Ford got up and said: "Before we close this meeting I would like to say that I hear a strange message. I seem to get the words 'The Three Musketeers.' Now I get some initials. The initials are A. J. B. Is there anyone in this audience who would recognize or have any connection with anything I have said? Certainly I do not."

Now as it happened, when the meeting was about to close, I had let up on my concentration. I said, "Well, this is it— nothing happened." So I just let go. It appears to be about that time things began to happen so far as Ford was concerned. I was about to answer Mr. Ford's question when he said, "I have something more. This voice reveals that the person who is being sought is in this audience. He is further to be found as a young man, that is to say, a man short of forty years, who is a clergyman, a clergyman in one of our Evangelical churches. The further message I have is, that A. J. B. wants him to know that he is quite happy where he is, that he does not get any spots and does not have to walk them off on Saturday morning. And that the person whom he is addressing would instantly understand the meaning of what he is saying." At this juncture Mr. Ford asked whether there was anybody who did recognize this somewhat confused message and I put up my hand. The meeting was then very late and no explanation was asked or given.

The following are the facts which go to explain something of the words that were spoken. Arthur J. Beyports was a young man who had come from York, Pennsylvania, the son of a merchant in that town. At Williamsport-Dickinson Seminary he and I had joined the same fraternity and played on the football team together. He was a large and strong young man and hence got the name of "Ajax." A fellow by the name of Herman Stackhouse who also played on the football team ran around with us a good deal. We were dubbed by many of our friends and many others on the campus as "The Three Musketeers," and among these we referred to Beyports as Ajax. Now, while I know that Ajax was not one of the names of the original three musketeers, that little discrepancy did not bother us.

In our last year at school, the president, one John Long, a Dickinson graduate, decided that the system of discipline, which we had, allowed for too much looseness, and he proposed a new system that would tighten up certain things which he felt needed tightening; to wit: for any more or less substantial default in the rules, we were given one demerit, and if we amassed five demerits by Friday night, we were not allowed to have Friday evening out, the one night of the week that was designated for recreation off the campus. Most of us, of course, saw to it that we kept under five, but that still gave us considerable latitude; that is to say, the bed might not be very well made, we might have a shoe out of place, or so on. In order to take care of this, Long suggested that the five demerits be broken down into what he called twenty-five spots, or five spots for one demerit. Thereby, the professors who inspected our rooms could give us a spot for a wrinkled bed or a spot for being late to class, or a spot for a shoe out of place. Of course it was our business to keep ourselves under twenty-five, which we did. But then what did you do about the man who got the twenty-three or twenty-four spots? Did he get off scot-free? Well, under the rules, he did. But then Long thought of another wrinkle and that was to require us to put a gun in hand and walk with the gun in the manner of a soldier before the gymnasium for fifteen minutes for each spot. Well, this was the straw that broke the camel's back, and most of us in the senior class, including particularly Stackhouse, Beyports, and myself, refused to do it and almost left school at the time. It was remembered by us as the "great revolution," having to do with the "spots." Therefore, the word that came, "We don't get any spots here and don't have to walk them off on Saturday morning," would indicate a particular reference to a particular time and circumstance.

This is about the substance of the story and it had to me at the time a highly evidential value because of the triteness, shall we say, of the information and yet the very fact of this triteness, because it was so completely verifiable in my experience, indicated that the occasion was more than a happenstance.

This is a very interesting story that my friend Dr. Horlacher tells. As *evidence,* however, it can be criticized in one important respect—there is an *alternative explanation* to be considered. The alternative explanation is *telepathy.* I do not believe that this was the case, but it can conceivably be argued that the medium, Mr. Ford, did not get his information from the deceased Beyports, but from *reading the mind* of Dr. Horlacher.

To rule out telepathy as an explanation of most of the phenomena of mediumship it is necessary to find cases in which the communicated material is not only unknown to the person receiving the communication (Dr. Horlacher in the above instance) but unknown to any *one* living person. This does not rule out telepathy completely, for it may be possible for the medium to fish about telepathically in the minds of persons who are not present and piece together the bits of information thus obtained, but it does greatly reduce the range of the telepathic hypothesis. Even if the medium could do this, it would be tremendously difficult, and there is no good evidence that it can be done at all. But the possibility of it must be considered, no matter how remote. Here is an illustration from the files of the Society for Psychical Research that, since the information received was unknown to any single person, seems to reduce the telepathic hypothesis almost to a vanishing point.* It is called "The Case of Daisy's Second Father."

*"On a Series of Sittings with Mrs. Osborne Leonard," by Miss Radclyffe-Hall and [Una] Lady Troubridge, *Proceedings of the Society for Psychical Research* [London], Vol. XXX [1919], pp. 521-46.

Miss Radclyffe-Hall had a friend, Daisy Armstrong, whose husband had been killed in World War I. Daisy wrote from the Near East to ask Miss Radclyffe-Hall if she would consult the famous trance-medium, Mrs. Osborne Leonard, in London, and try to get some news of her husband through Mrs. Leonard. Miss Radclyffe-Hall wrote back that she "would await a favorable opportunity." A few days later, Miss Radclyffe-Hall was "sitting" with Mrs. Leonard when contact was established with "AVB," a person who in life had been friendly with Daisy Armstrong. The contact was established through Feda, one of Mrs. Leonard's controls—supposed to be the spirit of a little girl. Miss Radclyffe-Hall then asked AVB (through Feda) if she "remembered an old friend of mine called Daisy." AVB replied that she did remember Daisy. She then indicated that there were two men present (in the spirit world) who wanted to communicate with Daisy, and that she (AVB) had known one of these men herself during her lifetime, but not the other. Nothing more of interest happened at this sitting, but at later sittings it was made clear that the two men purported to be Daisy's husband and father. AVB had known the husband when she was alive, but not the father.

At the first sittings, nothing was given which was not within the knowledge of Miss Radclyffe-Hall, the sitter. But at a later sitting, a number of details about Daisy's father were given, most of them unknown to Miss Radclyffe-Hall. For instance, an "old hat" was accurately described. Although Daisy herself, when apprised of this, had a faint memory of such a hat, it was her sister who recalled that the father had a favorite hat that was known in the family as "the old hat," and that he was in the habit of remarking: "You will spoil my afternoon if you won't let me wear the old hat!" There were many other references to past events and people which were later verified either by Daisy or her sister. Then at one sitting, Daisy's father said: "There were two of us who stood in the same relation to Daisy, with a slight difference. . . . Do you follow me?" Feda had referred just before this to a man "writing in jerks," and had described at length a machine in this man's room: "It's nearly all made of some dark-colored metal . . . a big thing on a stand . . . like a rolly thing or a rod running through the middle, two narrower rods as well, and above the rods something seems to rise up, something that looks curved." All of this Daisy Armstrong, in the Near East, recognized as applying perfectly to her *adopted father*, the Reverend Bertrand Wilson, *whom she believed to be alive in England*. But it was subsequently learned that he had *died three days before this sitting had taken place*. The adopted father was a composer and was in the habit of sitting all day at his table, composing music. In the next room he had a printing press. The investigators (Miss Radclyffe-Hall and Lady Troubridge) wrote: "An inspection of the Excelsior Model Hand-Printing Machines has revealed that Feda's description of the machine was very near the mark indeed." Neither of the investigators knew that Daisy had an adopted father—Miss Radclyffe-Hall had not seen her for many years and Lady Troubridge had never met her, nor did they know that such a person as the Reverend Mr. Wilson existed. A perfect stranger to the entire group had to be contacted in order to find out the exact date of the adopted father's death.

Here, then, would seem to be a case which very nearly rules out the telepathic hypothesis. The facts that came out *were* facts, and they were unknown to the medium, the sitter, or to any other one person, including Miss Daisy Armstrong.

Another medium whose reputation for honesty is unquestioned is Mrs. Eileen Garrett, publisher of magazines and books, and a well-known figure in psychical research. Mrs. Garrett has been "tested" both in England and the United States any number of times, and has worked with Dr. J. B. Rhine at Duke University, with Dr. Gardner Murphy at City College of New York, and with Mr. Harry Price in London.

Mrs. Garrett first came into prominence when the airship R-101 crashed in flames near Beauvais, France, in the early morning of Sunday, October 5, 1930. The ship's commander, Flight-Lieutenant H. C. Irwin, died in the wreck.

On Thursday, October 2, Dr. Price had made an appointment with Mrs. Garrett for a séance in his laboratory in London the following Tuesday afternoon, October 7. This was two days after the wreck of the R-101. As soon as Mrs. Garrett had gone into trance her spirit control, Uvani, stand that Lieutenant Irwin wished to communicate. Mrs. Garrett's voice suddenly changed and "Irwin" poured out a detailed and highly technical account of how the airship crashed. At a subsequent public inquiry, presided over by Home Secretary

Sir John Simon, many of "Irwin's" statements were found to be correct.*

The following séance utterances were *proved to be facts:*

Bulk of the dirigible was too much for her engine capacity. . . . Engines too heavy. . . . Useful lift too small. . . . Gross lift computed badly. . . . Elevator jammed (probable). . . . Flying too low altitude. . . . Load too great for long flight. . . . Cruising speed bad and ship badly swinging. . . . Severe tension on fabric, which is chafing. . . . Starboard strakes started. . . . Never reached cruising altitude. . . . Airscrews too small (probable). . . . Impossible to rise. . . . Cannot trim.

"Irwin" made a great many other comments.

During the séance Mrs. Garrett, or "Irwin," made one remarkable statement. She said: "This exorbitant scheme of carbon and hydrogen is entirely and absolutely wrong." At the time of the R-101 flight a series of experiments was being contemplated in which hydrocarbon (a mixture of hydrogen and fuel oil) would be used as fuel, with the hydrogen being obtained from the gas bags of the airship and the carbon from the ship's supply of fuel oil. The experiments were "top secret," and were unknown outside of official circles. To have the scheme suddenly revealed by a medium was rather startling.

"Irwin" also said that "We almost scraped the roofs at Achy." Achy is a tiny village twelve and a half miles north of Beauvais and was not mentioned in any press reports of the disaster. It was not named in any guidebook, or on the ordinary maps of France. But it *was* discovered on the special large-scale ordnance flying maps similar to the one Lieutenant Irwin was using on the ill-fated ship. At the official inquiry, two French officers stated that when the airship passed over Poix (fourteen miles north of Achy), she was only three hundred feet from the ground—thus apparently lending confirmation to the séance story.

Price concluded that it would have been impossible for Mrs. Garrett to have obtained the information she possessed

*Mrs. Garrett had previously had a vision of the ship's crashing, and had gone to the Home Secretary in an attempt to get him to cancel the flight. He had refused, stating that if he canceled it everybody would say that the British Government was "being run by spooks." But Count Eckner, designer of the aircraft, later said if the vision had been called to his attention he would not have permitted the ship to leave the ground.

normally, and stated it as his opinion that the case strongly supports the hypothesis of survival.

All of this sounds convincing. Evidence like this was good enough to persuade many intelligent men and women of the truth of survival. Some of it, indeed, seems irrefutable on any grounds. But to the scientist it suffers from one drawback—it cannot be analyzed and graded *statistically*. How shall the element of chance be ruled out?

To the person who is already convinced of the truth of survival, this seems like a petty criticism. Besides, the phenomena of psychical research do not lend themselves readily to any kind of statistical evaluation. But, realizing that this is a criticism which is valid for science, a number of parapsychologists have tried to work out methods whereby mediumistic phenomena may be analyzed statistically.

Perhaps the best of these methods is the one worked out by Dr. J. G. Pratt while on the staff of the Duke University Parapsychology Laboratory. Dr. Pratt's method calls for collecting the medium's statements verbatim in sets of five or more sittings, each sitting being with a different subject. The subject, as a rule, is not present at the sitting in person but is represented by a token that once belonged to a deceased friend with whom he is trying to communicate—a watch, a ring, a fountain pen, or some such.

The records of these "token" sittings are copied in quintuplicate and a set of all five records, with no identification except a code number, is given to each subject who has sent a token. When each of the five subjects has checked all the records, making note of the statements that seem to pertain to him, he is given a copy of his own record. The records are then evaluated statistically. The method, foolproof from a statistical point of view, shows results far in excess of what might be expected from pure chance. In two series of sittings which Dr. Pratt conducted with Mrs. Eileen Garrett at Duke, odds of 1,700,000 to 1 against chance were obtained! In the future other mediums will be tested by Dr. Pratt's method.

How conclusive is the evidence of survival obtained through mediumship? Not conclusive perhaps, but very good, and getting better as methods of evaluating mediumship statistically are worked out at Duke and elsewhere. Such evidence as has been cited here simply cannot be ignored or laughed off; it was good enough to convince some of the finest minds in science and psychology of the truth of survival. Discount the fakers, the frauds, and the charlatans as you will (and they greatly outnumber the honest mediums); you still have a small residue of truth, a tiny area of incontrovertible fact, in which to plant the seeds of man's hope for eternal life. As William James said—it takes only one white crow to prove that not all crows are black.

Do you know who you are?
—Dostoevski

3

THE STRANGE CASE
OF SALLY BEAUCHAMP

TODAY THERE ARE TWO RELATED SCIENCES THAT ARE exploring the mind. They are psychology, which approaches the mind from the physical side, and *para*psychology, or psychical research, which approaches it from the nonmaterial side. And somewhere deep down in the depths there is a shadowy no-man's land where depth psychology and psychical research share a common frontier. Somewhere along that undefinable boundary there is buried treasure, a vein of pure gold. Now and then the picks of the scientific prospectors touch it and turn up rare nuggets.

One such nugget, as shining and mysterious as it was when news of it was the sensation of the learned societies, is the strange case of the Beauchamp family.

One day in the year 1898 a new patient presented herself to Dr. Morton Prince, the eminent psychologist who was a professor at Tufts Medical School and consulting physician at the Boston City Hospital. Her name was Christine L. Beauchamp; she was twenty-three years old and a student at a women's college near Boston. She was suffering from what was then called neurasthenia, but is today called merely neurosis, or nervous exhaustion. She was weak and listless, could not concentrate, suffered lapses of memory, was unstable emotionally, could not sleep—the usual symptoms of a rather ordinary case of "nerves."

When the customary methods of treatment failed to produce any improvement, Dr. Prince decided to try hypnotic suggestion. The patient passed easily into a light but well-marked hypnotic trance and in it could converse intelligently with Dr. Prince and was cognizant of her waking life, although on coming out of the hypnosis she remembered nothing that had taken place during it. She took the suggestion well and some improvement in her condition was noted.

One day she went into a hypnotic trance that was somewhat deeper than usual, and Dr. Prince was surprised to note that a new personality, utterly unlike the patient when she was hypnotized, was emerging. This personality spoke with a different voice; she stuttered (something the patient never did), appeared in good health, was brash and cheerful. The contrast between this personality and the timorous, weak, mournful patient was so amazing that the doctor was temporarily at a loss for words. The new personality, moreover, spoke of the patient as "she"; as someone completely separate from herself.

"But," said the doctor, "you are she."

"No, I am not."

"I say you are."

Silence. Then the doctor said: "But why are you not she?"

"Because she does not know the same things that I do."

"But you both have the same arms and legs, haven't you?"

"Yes, but arms and legs do not make us the same."

When the patient came out of the hypnosis she knew nothing of the new personality that had appeared. But again and again in the hypnotic trance the new personality would come, always strikingly different from the patient, always able to carry on conversations with the doctor that were considerably more helpful than those he had with the patient either in her ordinary waking state or in trance. The new personality first took the name of Chris and later called herself Sally. She was stubborn, mischievous, childlike. She had her own memories, her own characteristics. To differentiate between them the doctor called Sally B-3, and the patient's usual personality B-1. Soon Sally, who did not like B-1 because she was a weakling, was alternating with her not only in hypnosis but also in the waking state, taking charge of the body which she shared with B-1 for periods of hours or even days, during which time the patient (Miss Beauchamp, or B-1) would suffer complete amnesia. On such occasions, on coming to she would immediately phone Dr. Prince to tell him that she had "lost" so many hours or days and could remember nothing that had happened. During this lost period, of course, her body was being run by Sally or B-3, and run quite differently from the manner in which Miss Beauchamp would run it. Miss Beauchamp was a very proper person and loathed coarse behavior. Sally would take a malicious delight in wearing outlandish clothes, putting her feet up on the table, and smoking cigarettes (very daring in those days) and doing other things at which she knew the conservative Miss B. would be aghast. Then she would deliberately drop from consciousness, and the unhappy Miss Beauchamp would suddenly "come to" with her feet on the mantle and a cigarette in her mouth, wondering how she had got that way and what in the world was the matter with her. For, while Sally knew everything that B-1 did, B-1 was completely ignorant of Sally.

In contrast to B-1, Sally was very healthy. She despised B-1 for her ill health, and frequently forced the common body to tasks that were too much for it. On one occasion when Sally was in charge, she went on a long and vigorous hike out to Watertown, a Boston suburb. Once out there, Sally disappeared and the weak, nervous Miss Beauchamp (B-1) came back into possession of the body—tired, dusty, dispirited, and completely lacking the strength to get herself back. On the other hand, when Miss Beauchamp faded out of the picture and Sally came in, health came with her. The distraught, complaining neurotic would be replaced by the hearty, healthy, and confident imp.

On one occasion, Miss Beauchamp became so exhausted she had to go to the hospital to recuperate. She was planning a trip to Europe at the time, but it looked as if she would be too weak to go. Dr. Prince called the hospital to see how she was coming along. "Fine," said the nurse in charge. "She's sitting up, gay as a lark. She'll be able to go, all right." Suspicious, Dr. Prince asked to speak with the patient. He needed only to hear that cheerful, childlike, stuttering voice to know that Sally was in charge. Later, Dr. Prince elicited from Sally the information that she wanted very much to go to Europe and was afraid that if Miss Beauchamp remained in charge of the body there would be no trip. So she had taken over (being the stronger of the two personalities) and if Dr. Prince had not intervened, Sally would have gone to Europe, in complete charge. Dr. Prince thwarted this, and later Miss Beauchamp did recover enough to make the trip.

Sally was continually (in hypnotic trance) trying to rub her eyes and get them open so that she could "see." It was not fair for Miss Beauchamp to see and for her (Sally) not to see, she would complain. She was just as entitled to see as B-1 was. On such occasions, Dr. Prince would hold her hands. "It was as if some invisible stranger had hold of her arms and was trying to wrest them from my grasp," she said. One day Sally succeeded in getting her eyes open and from then on was much more often in control of the body.

Sally was extremely helpful to Dr. Prince. She claimed to have existed as long as Miss Beauchamp herself, and she could recall childhood events that Miss Beauchamp had forgotten. Sally even wrote her autobiography, a long, serious, and rather skillful document which she then hid, along with some other possessions of hers, in a box in the woods. And in all of this Sally indignantly denied that she was a part of Miss Beauchamp and insisted on her right to her own independent existence. "I am a spirit," she said.

"Bosh," said the doctor, somewhat uncertainly.

After about a year of this, with Miss Beauchamp, or B-1, and Sally, or B-3, alternating in control of their common body, still a third distinct personality appeared. Dr. Prince called it B-4. "B-4 seemed quite as much a real person as did the Miss Beauchamp whom we all knew"—that is, as B-1. Sally took an immediate dislike to B-4 and dubbed the new member of the family "the idiot." B-4, a very mature and responsible personality, reciprocated Sally's dislike and a sharp feud developed between them. At first Sally, who knew whatever was in B-1's mind, did not know what was in B-4's. Later, however, the enterprising Sally got so she could read B-4's mind as well as she could Miss Beauchamp's, and when this happened she disliked her to the point of hatred.

The manner of B-4's coming to the "family" (as Dr. Prince now called his three Beauchamp personalities) was interesting. The lady of the house where the patient was boarding called the doctor one night to say that Miss Beauchamp was highly nervous, and wondered if he would drop by that evening and try to calm her. This Dr. Prince did. Miss Beauchamp, nervous, timid, and distraught as usual, met him at the door and ushered him into the living room. They talked for a few moments, and then there was a period of silence. As the doctor watched her a change came over Miss Beauchamp. She became composed and competent, her nervousness fell away, and when she spoke to him it was as if to a stranger. He had come in through a window, she said, and his name was Jones. He insisted that she, herself, had just let him in by way of the front door, and that he was Dr. Morton Prince. But she insisted that he was Jones and that he had been very foolish to come. The doctor, recognizing the presence of another personality, played along. Later B-4 receded and B-1, or Miss Beauchamp, came back, resumed her distraught air, recognized him as Dr. Prince, and ushered him out. The next day the new personality appeared in hypnosis and from then on was a regular member of the family. Poor Miss Beauchamp would start out for the doctor's office as B-1, would be metamorphosed on the way into the impish Sally, would enter as the mature and competent B-4, and leave as B-1 again, to suffer the same alternations of personality on the way home. Her life was thus a mixture of nervous and unstable periods of consciousness mixed with terrifying blackouts of which she could later remember nothing but of which she had intriguing reminders in the form of letters written to her by Sally or phone calls from unknown people who, as Sally or B-4, she had asked to call her.

On one occasion Miss Beauchamp decided to go to New York and get work in order to recoup her dwindling finances. For some reason, however, she got off the train at New Haven instead of continuing on to New York, and got a job as a waitress in a hotel dining room. B-1 did not care particularly for the job, as it taxed her strength, but her employers liked her and were kind. B-3 (Sally) was enthusiastic and when she was in control had a jolly time with the customers and her employers. B-4, however, hated the job. It was too menial. The employers were somewhat perplexed by the sudden changes in mood and appearance of the new waitress, but apparently did not notice too much amiss. One day, however, when B-4 had gained the ascendancy, she abruptly quit the position, demanded the little money she had coming, and ordered the elevator boy to call her a hack. After she had paid for the hack at the railroad station, there was not enough money left to get to Boston. So B-4 pawned Miss Beauchamp's watch, and the family left for Boston. On the way Sally got back into control, and when Boston was reached, Sally promptly rented a room instead of going back to Miss Beauchamp's old quarters. So when Miss Beauchamp (B-1) finally came back into control, she was lying on a bed in a strange room, remembering nothing that had happened since she had gone to bed in New Haven the previous night. Later Sally, who by now was able to read B-4's mind, told Dr. Prince about the watch, and on a subsequent trip to New Haven he was able to redeem it.

The sudden alternations of the three personalities made the patient's life a burden almost too great to be borne. She would take a bath and prepare herself for bed as B-4. Then, as she got into bed, B-1 would take over, and knowing nothing about the previous bath, would take another. Sally, knowing what was in the minds of both B-1 and B-4 might then come in, and, although she knew two baths had already been taken, might insist on another just for fun. On one occasion Sally took all the bedclothes and piled them in a heap on the floor in order to irritate the neat B-4. But B-4, quite capable of fencing with Sally, ignored the bedclothes and rolled up for the night in a steamer rug. In the morning Miss Beauchamp (B-1) woke to find herself inexplicably on the floor instead of in bed, with the room in complete disorder.

Gradually Dr. Prince began to bring some order out of this chaos. B-4, he discovered, knew nothing of the life of the patient for the past eight years, but was skillful in concealing this lack of knowledge. B-4 had memories beyond that eight-year period, but for the eight years just before the night that B-4 had first appeared on the occasion of Dr. Prince's visit to Miss Beauchamp's apartment, she had no memory. Sally, however, did have a memory covering these years and she was able to tell Dr. Prince about an event that had occurred eight years before that probably accounted for B-4's lack of memory, and also for the odd way in which B-4 had appeared for the first time. Eight years before, Miss Beauchamp had been a nurse in a Providence hospital; she had a gentleman friend by the name of Jones who had climbed a ladder up to her third-floor room at the hospital and looked in on her, frightening her half to death. Later that evening Jones had tried to kiss her. This was why, when B-4 first appeared, she had gone back to that traumatic event (which doesn't seem like much today, but had quite an effect on a shy girl sixty years ago) and had called Dr. Prince "Jones" and had insisted that he had entered via the window.

Dr. Prince also discovered that while B-1 and B-4 were quite different personalities when awake, they became the same personality when hypnotized. So B-1 hypnotized and B-4 hypnotized became known as B-2, and it was finally decided that B-2, a synthesis of B-1 and B-4, was the *real* Miss Beauchamp.

This meant, of course, that B-1 and B-4 had to be gradually merged through hypnotic suggestion, and that Sally had to be suppressed entirely. When Dr. Prince broke the news to Sally she resisted strenuously. "I won't, I won't! I won't be dead!" she cried. "I have as much right to live as she [B-1] has!" The doctor had a long argument with her, and was sorry to have to "murder" her—she was by far the healthiest and brightest of the family. As a matter of fact, he soon discovered that he could not "murder" her—she was too strong. He finally argued her into going back "to wherever she came from," which she finally did. After many relapses, the B-2 personality, first achieved only in hypnosis, was achieved also when the patient was awake, and this became the final "Miss Beauchamp."

What is to be said of this case? B-1 and B-4 can be explained on the grounds of dissociation of personality; when B-2 became the "real" Miss Beauchamp, she remembered the times when she had been B-1 and B-4, *but had no memory at all of the times when Sally or B-3 had been in charge*. Moreover, while accepting B-1 and B-4 as parts of herself, she indignantly repudiated the idea that Sally was any true part of her. Yet Sally was the dominant alternating personality— capable of being fully conscious, capable of reasoning, capable of experiencing emotion, capable of volition, and with a complete memory. Sally, however, was excluded from the final synthesis; she had indeed "gone back where she came from."

How explain Sally? Dr. William McDougall, perhaps the greatest psychologist this country has known, concluded that she was a *soul, a psychic entity, a spirit,* and gave it as his opinion that the Beauchamp Case showed clearly that "the normal personality consists of body and soul in interaction, the soul being not dependent upon the brain or other physical basis for its memory, but having the faculty of retaining and remembering among its other faculties." Moreover, he stated, such cases as this "went far to justify the belief in the survival of the human personality after the death of the body."

4

THE MOVING
FINGER WRITES

SOME OF THE MOST INTRIGUING EVIDENCE WE HAVE OF the survival of the human personality after death comes from automatic writing and automatic speech. The automatists are not mediums in the usual sense and do not go into trance, although some slight dissociation from their surroundings appears in most cases. "Automatic" phenomena are of two types, written and spoken. In the former, the automatist simply sits down and writes whatever comes to mind, and in the latter speaks it with someone else taking it down. The process is not fundamentally different from that which takes place on the psychiatrist's couch, where the patient simply rambles on, with one idea leading to another, and the doctor makes notes on what seems to him significant. The association-of-ideas test in psychology, where the subject writes a word like "father" and then follows it with a series of words suggested by that word, is really an automatism. The simplest form of automatism is a ouija board; the most complex is psychoanalysis. In all automatism from the ouija board to psychoanalysis the material is being dredged up from the subject's subconscious or subliminal mind, and the only argument between parapsychologists and psychical researchers on the one hand and psychiatrists and psychoanalysts on the other is on the question of how the material happens to be in the subliminal consciousness—is it there normally, or paranormally? With particular reference to the survival-after-death question, is the spirit which appears to be communicating through the automatism *really* the spirit of a deceased human being and therefore evidence of life after death, or is it merely the product of a dissociation of the subject's normal personality? This, of course, was the crux of the Beauchamp Case, with McDougall inclining strongly toward the spirit hypothesis. Perhaps a look at some interesting automatic phenomena will throw some light on the question.

Automatism is much too prosaic for the professional medium as a rule, so many of the outstanding automatists have been amateurs. One of the leading amateur automatists was Mrs. John H. Curran, wife of the immigration commissioner of Missouri, who was studied intensively by Dr. Walter Franklin Prince (no relation to Dr. Morton Prince), an Episcopal minister-turned-psychologist, who was for many years research officer of the American Society for Psychical Research. Mrs. Curran was also the subject of a book by Casper S. Yost, a newspaperman who at first thought Mrs. Curran was a fraud, but ended up as one of her staunchest supporters.*

Mrs. Curran was an average upper-middle-class housewife, and had no particular interest in psychical research. In the year 1913, however, the ouija board was the latest "rage," and she, like a lot of other people, bought one. On a hot July evening, she and a friend, Mrs. Emily Grant Hutchings, were playing with the new toy at the Currans' home in St. Louis. They had "sat" with it before, but had never had any luck. But on this particular evening (they were waiting for their husbands to come home from some meeting) the little wooden pointer on the ouija board began to move rapidly and definitely from one letter to another, spelling out a strange message:

> Many moons ago I lived. Again I come. Patience Worth my name.

The women looked at one another in astonishment. The pointer flew about the board again:

> Wait, I would speak with thee. If thou shalt live, then so shall I. I make my bread by thy hearth. Good friends, let us be merrie. The time for work is past. Let the tabbie drowse and blink her wisdom to the fire-log.

"How quaint!" exclaimed Mrs. Hutchings.
The board replied snappily:

*Casper S. Yost, *Patience Worth* [New York: Henry Holt & Co., 1916].

Good Mother Wisdom is too harsh for thee and thou should'st love her only as a foster-mother.

That was the beginning of "Patience Worth." From then on, over a period of years, Patience poured a stream of communications through the ouija board, operated by Mrs. Curran. There were epigrams, conversations, poems, stories, allegories—all in seventeenth-century English, all beautifully constructed and historically accurate. Two of the stories were actually published in novel form by Henry Holt and Co.!

Patience had a sharp wit. On one occasion, the Currans had a skeptical young physician and his wife as dinner guests, and after dinner the two ladies wooed Patience via the ouija board while the men watched. The doctor remarked: "I hope Patience Worth will come. I'd like to find out what her game is."

Immediately the pointer flew about the board beneath the fingers of the women, and Patience asked tartly: "Dost then desire the plucking of another goose?"

DOCTOR. By George, she's right there with the grease, isn't she?

PATIENCE. Enough to baste the last upon the spit.

DOCTOR. Well, that's quick wit for you. Pretty hard to catch her.

PATIENCE. The salt of today will not serve to catch the bird of tomorrow.

DOCTOR. She'd better call herself the bird of yesterday. I wonder what kind of a mind she had, anyway?

PATIENCE. Dost crave to taste the sauce?

DOCTOR. She holds to her simile of the goose. I wish you'd ask her how she makes that little table move under your hands to spell the words.

PATIENCE. A wise cook telleth not the brew.

DOCTOR. Turn that board over and let me see what's underneath it.

(*The board was turned over and duly inspected.*)

PATIENCE. Thee'lt bump thy nose to look within the hopper.

DOCTOR. Whew! She doesn't mind handing you one, does she?

DOCTOR'S WIFE. That's Patience's way. She doesn't think we count for anything.

PATIENCE. The bell-cow doth deem the good folk go to Sabbath house from the ringing of her bell.

DOCTOR. She evidently thinks we are a conceited lot. Well, I believe she'll agree with me that you can't go far in this world without a fair opinion of yourself.

PATIENCE. So the donkey loveth his bray!

DOCTOR'S WIFE. You can draw her on all you please. I'm going to keep still.

PATIENCE. Oh, e'en the mouse will have a nibble.

So much for Patience's quick and astringent wit. Her literary production was of the same high quality as her conversation. Here is a sample of her poetry:

> *Ah, God, I have drunk unto the dregs,*
> *And flung the cup at Thee!*
> *The dust of crumbled righteousness*
> *Hath dried and soaked unto itself*
> *E'en the drop I spilled to Bacchus,*
> *Whilst Thou, all-patient,*
> *Sendest purple vintage for a later harvest.*

This is a verse that might well be included in any anthology of seventeenth century poetry. Patience, through the ouija board, turned out literally thousands of lines of it.

At first, it was believed that Patience Worth was really some part of the subconsciousness of Mrs. Hutchings, who was a writer of modest ability. However, it soon developed that it was Mrs. Curran, and not Mrs. Hutchings, through whom Patience was working. Patience was never in evidence unless Mrs. Curran was at the board, but Mrs. Hutchings' absence made no difference at all. As for Mrs. Curran, she had no literary pretentions, and only a cursory knowledge of English history. She was fairly intelligent, but the intelligence manifest in Patience Worth's work went far beyond hers. There was no séance hocus-pocus connected with the sittings in the Curran home; the lights were on and the entire thing took place with the eyes of all present focused on the board. Mrs. Curran herself was decidedly taken aback by the whole thing, could not explain it, and was afraid that if word of it got out people would think she was "queer." She had a horror of being thought of as any sort of medium.

Many psychologists came to St. Louis to study Mrs. Curran and Patience Worth, and as usual they disagreed about the case. Was Patience Worth really the surviving spirit of an intelligent Englishwoman who had lived in the seventeenth century, or merely a buried or dissociated part of Mrs. Curran's personality which had found an outlet via the ouija board? To affirm the latter, of course, still did not answer the basic question: what is the *intelligence* behind the board that directed the phenomena? It was generally agreed that it was an intelligence considerably beyond that of the normal, conscious Mrs. Curran.

Dr. Walter Franklin Prince, who worked more intensively on the case than any other psychologist, summed it up by saying that "either our concept of what we call the subconscious must be radically altered so as to include potentialities of which we hitherto have had no knowledge, or else some cause operating in the subconsciousness of Mrs. Curran must be acknowledged."*

Patience Worth is a good example of the simplest type of automatism. A more complex kind of automatic writing and speech is found in the work of a group of talented amateur automatists, members of the English Society for Psychical Research. The three principal members of this group were Mrs. A. W. Verrall, a lecturer at Newnham College and the wife of a well-known Cambridge University classicist; and two ladies who preferred to hide their lights under the pseudonyms, "Mrs. Willett," and "Mrs. Holland." These women, all of the highest integrity, "sat for script" with each other and with different members of the Society for Psychical Research. Soon after the deaths of such older researchers as Frederic W. H. Myers, Edmund Gurney, and Richard Hodgson, messages purporting to be from these worthies appeared in the scripts (either written down or dictated) of Mrs. Verrall, Mrs. Willett, and Mrs. Holland.

Now automatic writing, like the apparently random observations by the patient on the psychoanalyst's couch, needs interpreting. Since it comes without deliberation and is more or less a product of free association, it will inevitably contain a lot of gibberish that the conscious mind would rule out if it were in control of the process. Indeed, the value of the whole thing—as in psychoanalysis—is that the conscious mind is *not* in control. So the automatists write and speak a lot of guff which must be winnowed carefully for something of value— just as you would speak if you let your tongue "run with the belt off," and said whatever came into your mind. Sometimes they even "automatize" in languages which their conscious minds do not know; the references in the Bible to the Tower

---

*For a full account of this extraordinary case, see Dr. W. F. Prince's *The Case of Patience Worth* [Boston Society for Psychical Research, 1927]. For a briefer account, see the chapter entitled "The Coming of Patience Worth," Alson J. Smith, *The Psychic Source-Book* [New York: Creative Age Press, 1951].

of Babel and "speaking with tongues" are examples of mass automatism.

When the conscious mind is in control of our voices and hands it does not permit us to speak or write nonsense or anything that is socially unacceptable. It is a censor which dictates what we shall or shall not say or write. In automatism, as in psychoanalysis, the censorship of the conscious mind is suppressed and the voice or the hand is free to express whatever may bubble up from the subconscious. Much of it will be nonsense (and the psychoanalysts tell us that a good deal of it will be socially unacceptable!). The question here is: is it possible for those who are no longer in this life to communicate with us through our subconscious minds? And can these communications, which would ordinarily be censored out by our conscious minds, appear in the apparent gibberish that comes up from the subconsciousness and gets expression (in automatic speech and writing) when the conscious censor is temporarily off guard?

But, you may say, the automatist is not asleep or in trance. How then can you say that the conscious censor is not operating? The answer to that is (1) there is usually some dissociation present in automatism even though the automatists are not in trance; there is a distinct *absent-mindedness*, an unawareness of surroundings, an intense concentration; (2) to turn again to the analogy with the psychoanalytic technique: it is possible, by an act of will, a deliberate relaxation, to temporarily and consciously circumvent the censor. This is what the patient on the psychoanalyst's couch does when he allows his mind to follow the "free association" process.

Bearing this in mind, let us look at some of the evidence obtained through automatic speech and writing.

A number of years ago Mr. J. G. Piddington of the Society for Psychical Research wrote a letter which was not to be opened until after his death. He then sealed it and put it away in a safe to which only he had access. In the letter he commented on his tendency, both as a child and as an adult, to play constantly with the number seven. He counted railroad cars in groups of seven, counted up to seven before making a decision, walked in a seven-step rhythm, etc. In psychology this is known as a "tic," and Piddington referred to it as a tic in his "posthumous" letter. Piddington said nothing to anyone about the letter.

Three years later, with the letter still reposing unopened in the safe and Piddington still alive, the automatists—Mrs. Verrall, Mrs. Holland, and Mrs. Piper (who was an automatist as well as a trance medium) began to get a lot of references to "seven" in their scripts. The phrase "we are seven" appeared, and also constant references to the clock with its "tick, tick." So often did the references to "seven" and to "tick" appear that it was obvious that they had some significance. Finally Piddington revealed the contents of his letter.

How account for this? Had the mind of Piddington leaked the information telepathically to the automatists? Or had they exercised clairvoyance to see the contents of the sealed letter in the safe?

Both of these possibilities are intriguing in themselves, but there was still another and even more interesting possible explanation. At the same time that Piddington had been writing his "posthumous" letter in London, the automatic script of Mrs. Verrall in Cambridge had been full of messages that purported to come from Frederic W. H. Myers, who had died some time before. Even as Piddington wrote his letter, Mrs. Verrall had been writing: "Note the hour—in London half the message has come . . . surely Piddington will see that this is enough and should be acted upon." Later "Myers" wrote again through Mrs. Verrall: "Has Piddington found the bits of his sentence scattered among you all?" Remember, all this time Mrs. Verrall and the other automatists had no conscious knowledge that Piddington had written any letter at all. The third possibility, therefore, was that the appearance of bits of Piddington's letter in the scripts of the automatists was due to deliberate action on the part of a deceased personality (Myers) who had chosen this method of indicating his survival to his friends.

The above is a simple example of what is known in psychical research and parapsychology as *cross-correspondence*. The cross-correspondences are psychic jig-saw puzzles with various parts of the puzzle coming through in the scripts of different automatists and making no sense at all *until they are compared*. They then fit together and convey some sort of message. When thus brought together they show a single purpose and meaning, are indicative of careful planning by the alleged communicators, and are entirely characteristic of them.

Sir Oliver Lodge, who by then (1908) was one of England's outstanding psychical researchers, was very much interested in Piddington's "sevens" letter. Was it really Frederic W. H. Myers who was communicating through the scripts of the automatists and who had revealed the contents of Mr. Piddington's sealed letter? Sir Oliver worked out a test which would involve cross-correspondence. Mrs. Piper was in the United States at this time and Mrs. Willett was in England; any kind of collusion between the two was impossible. "Myers" was appearing in the automatic scripts of both women. So Sir Oliver wrote to his friend Mr. George B. Dorr in the United States and asked him to put this question to "Myers" through Mrs. Piper: "What does the word 'Lethe' mean to you?" At the same time Sir Oliver himself asked the same question of "Myers" through Mrs. Willett in England. The idea was that if "Myers" was just a dissociated, or a split-off part of the subconscious mind of either Mrs. Piper or Mrs. Willett, he would not know that the same question had been asked of him through the other lady. On the other hand, if he did show an awareness of the fact that he had been asked the same question twice, once through Mrs. Piper and once through Mrs. Willett, that would be strong evidence indeed that, whatever else he might be, he was definitely not a dissociated part of the personality or subconsciousness of either lady. Moreover, the question was one which it was peculiarly appropriate to ask of "Myers," who had been a classical scholar when alive, and an answer to it in any detail was quite beyond either Mrs. Piper or Mrs. Willett.

When Mr. Dorr, in the United States, asked this question of "Myers" communicating through Mrs. Piper, the result (in her automatic script) was a torrent of classical material, very much jumbled, which he could not understand. However, classical scholars in London went over the script and were able to pick out specific references to the little-known Story of Ceyx and Alcyone and the dispatching of the goddess Iris to the underworld. This is the story that is told at the end of Ovid's *Metamorphoses,* and the river Lethe figures in it. In its detail and deliberate obscurity it was an answer entirely characteristic of Frederic W. H. Myers, and one quite a bit beyond Mrs. Piper, who had never had a classical education.

A few days later the same question about Lethe was asked of "Myers" through Mrs. Willett in England, and immediately her script contained references to the fact that the same question had been asked elsewhere. With many signs of effort, the word "Dorr" was spelled out in Mrs. Willett's script—and George Dorr, you will remember, was the man who had asked the test question of "Myers" through Mrs. Piper in the United States. "Myers" then answered the question with a series of references to the sixth book of Vergil's *Aeneid* which were pertinent to the word "Lethe." Finally, as if to show he was completely aware of the whole scheme, "Myers" wrote through Mrs. Willett: "That I have different scribes means that I must show different aspects of thoughts underlying which Unity is to be found, and I know what Lodge wants. He wants me to prove that I have access to knowledge shown elsewhere."

In order that you may understand still more clearly just what a cross-correspondence is, let's look at this one, which is built around the word "arrow."

Feb. 11, 1907—Mrs. Verrall's script has a drawing of three converging arrows, followed by the words: *"Tria convergentia in unum."*

Feb. 12—The Spirit of Dr. Richard Hodgson, allegedly communicating through Mrs. Piper, says he had given "Arrow" to Mrs. Verrall.

Feb. 13—Mrs. J. G. Piddington of the SPR sees Mrs. Verrall's script of Feb. 11.

Feb. 17—The script of Mrs. Verrall's daughter has a drawing of an arrow, followed by the words "many together."

Feb. 18, about 11:15 A.M.—Mrs. Verrall's script has several words beginning with "a" and "ar," such as "architrave," "arch," etc.

Feb. 18, about 11:30 A.M.—"Hodgson," communicating through Mrs. Piper, reminds Mr. Piddington, who is sitting with Mrs. Piper, to "watch for arrow."

Feb. 19, about 10:55 A.M.—Mr. Piddington sees Mrs. Verrall's script of Feb. 18 and Miss Verrall's of Feb. 17.

Feb. 19, about 11:20 A.M.—"Hodgson," communicating through Mrs. Piper, says Mrs. Verrall wrote "ar" and "w."

Feb. 20—Mr. Piddington tells "Hodgson," through Mrs. Piper, that Mrs. Verrall has written several words beginning with "ar."

Feb. 25—"Hodgson," communicating through Mrs. Piper, asks: "Got arrow yet?" Mr. Piddington says Mrs. Verrall has not written the word, but has drawn an arrow. "Hodgson" says he will make a further attempt to make Mrs. Verrall write "arrow."

March 18—Mrs. Verrall's script has a drawing of a bow and arrow, an arrow, and a target.

June 4—Mrs. Verrall learns for the first time that "arrow" has been the subject of a cross-correspondence experiment.

Some of the cross-correspondences seem to show evidences of teamwork on the part of deceased individuals. They reveal deliberate planning, as though the collaborators had come together and decided to propound a psychic puzzle so characteristic of them that no one on the "other side" (the living) could doubt its authorship and that would dispose of the alternative explanations that skeptics could offer for the phenomena, namely that they were the result of the dissociation of the intermediary's personality, or the product of telepathic leaks from the minds of living people. Such psychic puzzles are necessarily quite complex and are not easy to read or understand. But taken as a group they are very good evidence for the survival of personality and intelligence beyond the grave. Two of the best are what are known as the "Hope, Star, and Browning" and the "Ear of Dionysius" cases. Both are long and involved and space prevents the outlining of more than one here. Let's look for a moment at the "Ear of Dionysius."*

The "Ear of Dionysius" is a grotto hewn in the solid rock at Syracuse. It opens on one of the stone quarries, and was used as a place of confinement for Athenian prisoners who fell into the hands of the victorious Syracusans after the failure of the siege of Syracuse, an event which has been graphically described by Thucydides. Later the quarries were again used as prisons by Dionysius, Tyrant of Syracuse. The grotto had certain acoustic properties which magnified the slightest sound, and Dionysius used it to overhear the conversations of the prisoners. Partly because of this and partly because of a resemblance to the interior of a donkey's ear, the grotto was known as *L'Orecchio di Dionisio,* or the Ear of Dionysius.

On August 26, 1910, Mrs. Willett "sat for script" with Mrs. Verrall. (In other words, Mrs. Willett was the automatist and Mrs. Verrall took down what she said.) The script was partly written and partly spoken, and in the spoken part of it there suddenly appeared the seemingly irrelevant phrase "Dionysius' Ear the lobe." The word "Dionysius" was given its Italian pronunciation. The phrase meant nothing at the time to either Mrs. Willett or Mrs. Verrall.

Three years went by without any other references to Dionysius and his grotto in the scripts of any of the automatists. Then, on the tenth of January, 1914, as Sir Oliver Lodge sat with Mrs. Willett, the automatist, the following passage appeared:

*For a full account see *The Psychic Source-Book,* or *Proceedings of the Society for Psychical Research* [London], Vol. XXIX [1918], pp. 197-243.

(EXTRACT FROM SCRIPT OF JANUARY 10, 1914.)

Do you remember you did not know and I complained of your classical ignorance IGNORANCE.

It concerned a place where slaves were kept—and Audition belongs, also Acoustics.

Think of the Whispering Gally.

To toil, a slave, the Tyrant—and it was called Orecchio—that's near.

One Ear, a one-eared place, not a one-horsed dawn (here the automatist laughed slightly), a one-eared place—you did not know (or remember) about it when it came up in conversation, and I said Well what is the use of a classical education—.

Where were the fields of Enna?

(Drawing of an ear)

an early pipe could be heard

To sail for Syracuse

Who beat the loud-sounding wave, who smote the moving furrows

The heel of the Boot

Dy Dy and then you think of Diana Dimorphism

To fly to find Euripides

not the Pauline Philemon

Now—at the beginning of the script it was stated that a message was to be sent to Mrs. Verrall, who was not present. When Mrs. Willett had sat with Mrs. Verrall back in 1910 and the phrase "Dionysius' Ear the lobe" had come through, Mrs. Verrall's husband, the eminent Cambridge classicist, A. W. Verrall, had been alive. She had asked him about the phrase, and he had explained to her that it was a place at Syracuse where Dionysius could overhear conversations, and had twitted her about her ignorance, saying: "What's the use of a classical education?" or words to that effect. *Dr. Verrall had since died.*

During his lifetime Dr. Verrall had delighted in intellectual puzzles of all kinds, and the above quotation and the ones which followed in the scripts of the automatists were entirely characteristic of him.

Now—the "place where slaves were kept" is a reference to the stone quarries where captives were imprisoned. The words that follow describe the "Ear of Dionysius" with its peculiar acoustic properties. The amusement recorded, "the automatist laughed slightly" is that of the communicator, who is recalling the incident in which he chided his wife (during his lifetime) for failing to get a classical allusion. The "fields of Enna" is a reference to the meadows in the town of Enna in Sicily which were famous in antiquity as the scene of the rape of Proserpina. The "early pipe" is evidently an allusion to Tennyson's:

> The earliest pipe of half-awaken'd birds
> To dying ears

Incidentally, the bringing of this poem into forced connection with the Ear of Dionysius by means of an abominable pun (the drawing of an ear to signify "early") is entirely characteristic of the alleged communicator, Dr. Verrall.

The next reference in the script is to the ill-fated Athenian expedition against Syracuse, and the words "who beat the loud-sounding wave, who smote the moving furrows," probably derive from Tennyson's *Ulysses:*

> Sitting well in order smite
> The sounding furrows.

The "heel of the Boot" doubtless refers to the route followed by the Athenian fleet, which passed from Corcyra to Tarentum, in the heel of Italy, coasted along the toe, and finally reached Sicily. "Dy Dy" is probably an attempt at the word "Dionysius"; the communicator, failing to get the whole word through to the automatist, then rebukes her for thinking the word begins with "Di" instead of "Dy." The final allusion in the script seems to have been taken from Browning's *Aristophanes' Apology or the Last Adventure of Balaustion:*

> I also loved
> The Poet, Free Athenai cheaply prized—
> King Dionusios,—Archelaos like.

Balaustion then asks Philemon "If he too have not made a votive verse" and Philemon replies:

> Grant, in good sooth, our great dead, all the same,
> Retain their sense, as certain wise men say,
> I'd hang myself—to see Euripides.

The automatist, incidentally, had never read *Aristophanes' Apology.*

Putting all this together and making some sense out of it

requires not only a classical education but a great deal of patience!

Interwoven with the classical allusions in the scripts which followed that of Mrs. Willett on January 10, 1914, were poetic references and allusions that were not characteristic of Dr. Verrall but that were very characteristic of a friend and colleague of his at Cambridge, Professor S. W. Butcher, who had died in 1910. Later in the scripts of Mrs. Willett and Mrs. Holland comes the information that the whole thing is a literary riddle, propounded by "two friends" who are identified as "Father Cam walking arm in arm with the Canongate" (Canongate was Edinburgh University; Butcher had taught there before coming to Cambridge). When the scripts of Mrs. Willett and Mrs. Holland were compared and analyzed not only by the psychical researchers but by unbiased classical scholars, the story told was that of Philoxenus, a friend of Dionysius the Elder, who became enamored of the beautiful flute-player Galatea, who was the mistress of Dionysius. Philoxenus was caught making love to Galatea and was imprisoned in the Ear of Dionysius, in the quarries. However, Dionysius was an amateur poet and Philoxenus was a scholar. So Dionysius released Philoxenus from prison to pass judgment on his poetry. After reading the tyrant's poems, Philoxenus cried out, "Take me back to the quarries!" Here he revenged himself by writing a dithyramb entitled "Cyclops," or "Galatea," in which he represented himself as Odysseus who, to take vengeance on Polyphemus (Dionysius), seduced the nymph Galatea.

All of this, over a period of years, came word by word, allusion by allusion, through the scripts of Mrs. Willett and Mrs. Holland (although the latter's contribution was limited to one message). No one script made much sense. It was only when the puzzle was painstakingly put together by researchers and scholars that it appeared in all its unity and beauty.

Obviously, such a puzzle had to be planned. Who planned it? "Verrall" and "Butcher"? It was entirely characteristic of them, and only two such scholars as they had been in life could have done it. Moreover, it was claimed in the scripts that they had indeed planned it as proof of their survival beyond the grave.

What are the alternative explanations? The first is that the puzzle was planned by living persons and the plan in all its detail transmitted *telepathically* to the automatists. The answer to this is that there was no living person from whose mind the essential elements utilized in the making of the puzzle can plausibly be supposed to have been supplied. Only six people saw the scripts at all. Moreover, there was no warrant in anything that was known then or is known today about telepathy for believing that the kind of particular and detailed information that was involved can be telepathically transmitted or received where no link already exists between the minds concerned in the process. Only two minds like those of Verrall and Butcher could have concocted such a puzzle. That there were two living minds comparable to theirs either consciously or unconsciously perpetrating such a fraud upon the automatists, or that there was one living mind which had the right combination of classical knowledge, poetic lore, and detailed memory of minutiae about A. W. Verrall and S. W. Butcher to create a puzzle and then work tirelessly over a period of years to get it telepathically into the minds of the automatists, is too great a strain on credulity.

A second possibility is that the whole thing came out of the subconscious minds of the automatists and is the product of the dissociation, or splitting off, of some part of their personalities. The answer here is that even a dissociated personality could not produce out of the subconscious something that was never there, and the combination of classical and poetic knowledge involved in the case was far, far beyond that of any of the good ladies involved. Nine-tenths of the puzzle came through Mrs. Willett, and she was a woman with no classical education whatever. Mrs. Verrall had some classical knowledge, but it was not comparable to that of her husband, and her role in the whole thing was more or less passive.

If we rule out fraud, telepathy, and dissociation of personality as explanations—and I think they should be ruled out—then we are left with no alternative but to accept the conclusion that the whole "Ear of Dionysius" communication had its source in some intelligence or intelligences not in the body. And if we accept that, we will not find any additional difficulty in believing that the "intelligences" were actually those of A. W. Verrall and S. W. Butcher.

A question that might well be asked is: why is everything so difficult, so obscure? Why didn't the communicators give the Dionysius part of the "Ear of Dionysius" puzzle to one automatist, the Polyphemus part to another, and so on?

The best answer to that is to admit that we don't know, and then to add that it is entirely possible that such an apparently simple process might actually be more difficult than the one followed. Mrs. Willett was an unusually good automatist, but even so it was difficult for the communicators to get the right word through her without false association. The associational networks of people differ; words mean different things. A word that the communicator might think would have a certain association in the mind of the automatist might turn out to have quite a different association and send her off on a wild-goose chase away from the idea that the communicator intended. It might then take hundreds or even thousands of words to get her back on the right associational path. If communication with the so-called "dead" is posssible at all, it is necessarily very difficult. It requires patience, intelligence, and perseverance, and many of the communications indicate a sense of acute frustration on the part of the communicators.

The cross-correspondences stand today among the very best evidences we have of the survival of the human personality, in intimate and recognizable form, beyond the experience we call death. The "Verrall" and "Butcher" who allegedly spoke from beyond the grave are, as we see them in "The Ear of Dionysius," the same warm, high-minded, intelligent men whom their friends knew on earth, with all the same idiosyncrasies and quirks of mind. And the cross-correspondences did not end with "The Ear of Dionysius." They are still going on today, and an intriguing case was reported as late as 1951 in the *Proceedings of the Society for Psychical Research*, London. Moreover, this is evidence that has not been and, indeed, cannot be challenged by science. In the face of it, science and orthodox psychology are silent. They do not deny the facts, and do not offer alternative explanations. But the new science of parapsychology accepts the cross-correspondences, and rates them with the best evidence we have for the survival of the individual human personality beyond the grave.

It was F. W. H. Myers, allegedly speaking from the "other side" through the automatic script of Mrs. Holland on January 12, 1904, who expressed the yearning of those who formulated the psychic puzzles:

> If it were possible for the soul to die back into earth-life again I should die from sheer yearning to reach you and to tell you that all that we imagined is not half wonderful enough for the truth. . . . Oh, I am feeble with eagerness—how can I best be identified?*

*Proceedings of the Society for Psychical Research [London], Vol. XXI [1910], pp. 233-34.

5

A GAMBIT FROM "THE OTHER SIDE"

AFTER ALL THE NONSENSE HAD BEEN WASHED OUT OF mediumship, after all the fakery had been duly weighed and discounted, there was a residue of good, honest evidence left. Mrs. Piper, Mrs. Soule, Mrs. Leonard, and Mrs. Garrett were "sensitives" (as they preferred to be called) who willingly, even enthusiastically, cooperated with men of science. They never evaded any test that the ingenious minds of researchers like William James, Richard Hodgson, Sir William Barrett, Lord Balfour, Sir Gilbert Murray, F. W. H. Myers, and J. B. Rhine could devise. The phenomena that they produced were subjected to all sorts of analysis, from infra-red rays to the probings of psychoanalysis and handwriting experts. They were shadowed by private detectives; their private lives were turned inside out and examined under the microscope. The findings were always in their favor. No imputation of fraud was ever brought against them.

The cross-correspondences and the phenomena produced by the automatists like Mrs. Curran, Mrs. Verrall, Mrs. Willett, and Mrs. Holland, went beyond the evidence from trance mediumship by reducing to an absolute minimum the *alternative hypotheses* to survival as explanations of the phenomena. The two alternative hypotheses most often advanced were, as we have seen: that (1) the phenomena were the result of the dissociation, or splitting off, of some part of the medium's normal personality; or (2) were due to telepathic leaks from human minds rather than to conscious effort by minds on the other side. The cross-correspondences completely discredited the former by showing that the information acquired could not possibly have been acquired normally by the automatist, and reduced the latter to absurdity by making the puzzle, or cross-correspondence, so complex and erudite that its being pieced together out of information fished telepathically from living minds was simply incomprehensible.

But "incomprehensible" and "absurd" are meaningless words to science. Science, like the United States Navy Sea-Bees in World War II, would boast that whatever was difficult it could do immediately, and whatever was impossible ("absurd" or "incomprehensible") would take a little longer. Telepathy-clairvoyance (generally considered in parapsychology as the same basic phenomenon, much as radio and television are fundamentally the same) was an "alternative explanation" that could be eliminated from all practical consideration without being *theoretically* eliminated—like the division of fractions in higher mathematics.

The best that could be done with this alternative hypothesis was to keep reducing it, even after it had already been reduced practically to the vanishing point. The last and best step in its reduction came with something which the psychical researchers called the "book tests." Telepathy from living minds did not seem to be even a remote possibility with the book tests, for the evidence offered through them was not known to any living person and substantiation for it came, not from pepole, but from documents. Like the cross-correspondences, the book tests were apparently initiated by intelligences not in the body as a sign of their continuing existence.

The tests began to appear sometime in 1917, in the mediumship of Mrs. Osborne Leonard in England.* They were carried on through trance mediums, and went something like this: the communicating spirit first identifies a particular bookcase in the sitter's house by mentioning its position in relation to the other furniture in the room—the door, the windows, etc. Usually the description will apply to one bookcase in the whole house. Then a particular shelf on this particular bookcase is mentioned—perhaps the third from the top—and a particular book on that shelf (third from the left, say) is singled out. The number of a page in that particular book is then given (say 217), and usually some indication as to the part of the page ("third paragraph") where a message of significance to the sitter will be found. The sitter then goes

*For a full description of the book tests, see Charles Drayton-Thomas, *Evidence for Human Survival* [London: W. Collins Sons Ltd., 1922]. For a shorter description, see *The Psychic Source-Book*.

home, searches the third shelf of the bookcase, picks up the third book from the left on that shelf, turns to page 217, the third paragraph, and reads something there that has a direct and personal meaning for him and for him alone.

The purpose of the book tests seems to be to send messages from the "dead" to the "living" in such form that they will be unintelligible, not only to the medium, but to the sitter and everybody else, until every clue is followed up and the message decoded, so to speak. Of course, for such tests to be valid, the medium must never have been in the sitter's home and must know nothing about his library. Unless this is true the whole thing is absurd (pardon me for using that word again!). But when it *is* true, the process is so highly evidential of survival beyond the grave that no alternative hypothesis can be offered except as the remotest of possibilities.*

A good illustration of a typical book test is this one, described by Mrs. Henry Sidgwick in the *Proceedings of the Society for Psychical Research,* London (Vol. XXXI). The sitter is a Mrs. Hugh Talbot, and the alleged communication is from her deceased husband:

Suddenly Feda (Mrs. Leonard's control) began a tiresome description of a book; she said it was leather and dark, and tried to show me (Mrs. Talbot) the size. Mrs. Leonard showed a length of eight to ten inches long with her hands, and four or five inches wide. She (Feda) said: "It is not exactly a book, it is not printed . . . it has writing in . . . there are two books, you will know the one he means by a diagram of languages in the front. . . . Indo-European, Aryan, Semitic languages. . . . A table of Arabian languages, Semitic languages." It sounded absolute rubbish to me. I had never heard of a diagram of languages and all these Eastern names jumbled together sounded like nothing at all, and she kept on repeating them and saying this is how I was to know the book, and kept on and on "Will you look at page 12 or 13. If it is there, it would interest him so much after this conversation." (In the earlier part of the sitting the communicator had repeatedly asked the sitter to believe that life continued after death and he did not feel changed at all.)

*If it be said that some kind of *clairvoyance* is an alternative possibility, then that in itself is a phenomenon so portentous in its implications for the overcoming of the time-space barrier that it opens up new and even more promising avenues of evidence. But clairvoyance has not been established by parapsychology anywhere nearly as firmly as has telepathy, and is still generally considered merely a subspecie of telepathy.

. . . Mrs. Talbot reported that the next day she found two old note-books which had belonged to her husband and which she had never cared to open. A shabby black leather one corresponded in size to Feda's description. "To my utter astonishment, my eyes fell on the words, 'Table of Semitic or Syro-Arabian Languages,' and pulling out the leaf, which was a long, folded piece of paper pasted in, I saw on the other side 'General Table of the Aryan and Indo-European Languages.'" On page 13 of this note-book was an extract from an anonymous work entitled *Post Mortem*. It describes the sensations of a person who realizes that he is dead, and of his meeting with his deceased relatives.*

In 1921 Sir William Barrett, who had been professor of physics at the Royal Academy in Dublin and who was one of the founders of the Society for Psychical Research, was given a book test while sitting with Mrs. Osborne Leonard. During the trance, the spirit of Sir William's old friend F. W. H. Myers purported to speak through Feda. "Myers" said that there were some books on the right-hand side of a room upstairs in the Barrett house in Devonshire Place, London. (Mrs. Leonard had never visited the Barrett home and was entirely unfamiliar with its interior arrangements.) "Myers" then said that on the second shelf, four feet from the floor, in the fourth book counting from the left, at the top of page 78, there were some words which he wanted Sir William to take as a direct answer from himself on the problem of immortality. "Myers" then said (through the control, Feda): "Two or three books from this test book there are two books on matters in which Sir William used to be interested, but of late years has not been so interested. They are connected with studies of his youth; and he will have particular memories of them, as they will remind him of his younger days."

Sir William had no idea what books "Myers" was referring to, but on his return home he found that George Eliot's *Middlemarch* was in the exact position mentioned. Now, "Myers" had observed that while he could not get the exact title of the book, he got a sense of "progression" from it. The title of the Eliot book certainly indicated progression. On page 78 the first line read: "ay, ay, I remember—you'll see I've remembered 'em all." This fitted in with what "Myers" had said, because much of Sir William's work since Myers' death had been concerned with the question of immortality

Proceedings of the Society for Psychical Research [London], Vol. XXXI [1921], pp. 253-60.

and whether the so-called "dead" retained their memories of the living.

The most significant part of this particular test, however, was that which had to do with the sentence, "Two or three books from this test book there are two books on matters in which Sir William used to be interested." The second and third books from *Middlemarch* were two volumes entitled *Heat* and *Sound*, by a physicist named Tyndall. In his younger days Sir William had been Tyndall's assistant and had worked on the experiments described in the books. None of the other books in the Barrett house were even remotely connected with the test.

Now—Mrs. Osborne, the medium, had never been in the Barrett home and knew nothing of Sir William's early life. But F. W. H. Myers *had* been in the house many times and had been an intimate friend of his from youth!

The outstanding recorder of book tests is a British Methodist (Wesleyan) clergyman by the name of Charles Drayton-Thomas. His book *Some New Evidence for Human Survival* (Glasgow: W. Collins and Sons and Co. Ltd., 1922) lists in detail many successful tests. Among them are the following (the medium is Mrs. Leonard and the control Feda):

The alleged communicator was the deceased father of the Reverend Mr. Drayton-Thomas, who, in life, had also been a Wesleyan minister. During one sitting, the communicator spoke of knocks, or raps, by means of which he tried on occasion to make his presence known to his son. He had often tried, but seldom was able to make any sounds which could not be attributed to natural causes.

Shortly after this sitting, the Reverend Mr. Drayton-Thomas was at home one night when he heard certain rappings that seemed to be systematic, punctuated three times by a loud double-knock. Three days later he was again sitting with Mrs. Leonard when Feda announced that *she* had gone to the Drayton-Thomas' home and made the knocks at the behest of the deceased elder Drayton-Thomas. She had tried to spell out her name in Morse code. Then Feda volunteered the following information, purporting to come from the elder Drayton-Thomas:

"He thinks you will be amused by the following test. It is in a book behind your study door, the second shelf from the ground, the fifth book from the left end. Near the top of page 17 you will see words which serve to indicate what Feda was attempting to do when knocking in your room. Now that you are aware that it was Feda's attempt you will see the unmistakable bearing of these words upon it."

After the sitting the Reverend Mr. Drayton-Thomas went home and looked for the book mentioned. It turned out to be a volume of Shakespeare. The third line from the top of page 17 was from Act I, Scene 3, of *King Henry VI*, and it read: "I will not answer thee with words, but blows."

On another occasion, the alleged communicator said (through Feda): "In your study close to the door, the lowest shelf, take the sixth book from the left, and page 149; three-quarters down is a word conveying the meaning of falling back or stumbling."

When the book mentioned was checked, the following sentence was found about three-quarters of the way down on page 149: ". . . to whom a crucified Messiah was an insuperable stumblingblock."

At still another time, the following test took place:

Feda said (after describing location, title, and page of a certain book): "Near the top, say one-quarter down, you will see a reference to a religious change, and almost underneath it are words expressing what your father would have felt about such a change."

The book in question turned out to be *Dr. McLaren of Manchester,* and a quarter of the way down the page indicated were quotations from Dr. McLaren describing his conversion-experience. The words underneath, which Feda referred to as "expressing what your father would have felt about such a change" were: "This letter . . . supplies the keynote to his whole life." The elder Drayton-Thomas had felt very strongly that "conversion," in the old Wesleyan sense, was indeed the "keynote" to all of life.

Once, after having given the location of a certain bookshelf, Feda said:

"Count from left to right, the third book, and page 87. On this page, and on page 132 also, is something interesting to you and to your father. Page 87 has to do with 'hearing,' not ordinary hearing with the ear, but as from the spirit-world. The words refer to literal hearing: take them as a message from him about your hearing him now. They suggest communication."

The book turned out to be *The Early Story of Israel,* by E. L. Thomas. Page 87 recounted a legend concerning Aaron: "As they stripped Aaron, a silvery veil of cloud sank over him like a pall and covered him. Aaron seemed to be asleep. Then Moses said, 'My brother, what dost thou feel?' He answered feebly: 'The cloud surrounds me and bereaves me of all joy.' And the soul of Aaron was parted from his body.

As it went up, Moses cried once more: 'Alas, my brother, what dost thou feel?' And the soul replied: 'I feel such joy that I would it had come to me sooner.' "

Both themes mentioned by Feda, literal hearing and "spirit-hearing," are found in the passage.

Feda went on: "Page 132 is a kind of continuation of the above message. A reference to your mediumship, but slightly different from the 'hearing.' "

Page 132 contained a description of Gideon, when before the camp of the enemy, overhearing the telling of a dream. Thus in this latter passage there is reference to communication by *dream* and in the previous one reference to communication by *voice*. Both of these methods of communication were indeed "something of interest" to the Reverend Mr. Drayton-Thomas and his father.

One final illustration—during one sitting, Feda told the Reverend Mr. Drayton-Thomas: "The set of books near the door, right-hand corner, bottom shelf, first book, page 2, and about the middle, there find something he wishes you to take as a personal message from him to you.'

In the middle of page 2 of the first book on the bottom shelf was this paragraph: "At the close of the year 1767 the Earl of Buchan died triumphing in the faith of Christ. He had been in the habit of hearing Whitefield, the Wesleys, and others, at Bath, and had felt their ministry a blessing. His last words were 'happy, happy, happy!' "

So much for the book tests. They are still going on, and reports of them are made from time to time in the *Proceedings of the Society for Psychical Research*, London, and the *Journal of the American Society for Psychical Research*.

The reader will have to evaluate them for himself. They seem, as previously indicated, to rule out all the alternative hypotheses to survival as explanations, leaving only the inference that here, indeed, we have a *planning intelligence* on the other side of the veil revealing itself as unmistakably, and characteristically, as possible. With fraud, dissociation of personality on the part of the medium, and telepathy, canceled out as explanations of the phenomena, we are left with only *chance* as a faint possible alternative. Was the medium just making a series of lucky guesses? The odds against that, of course, are astronomical—almost beyond imagination.

To the Reverend Mr. Drayton-Thomas—a very intelligent and respected gentleman who is still living in England, by the way—the whole performance at first appeared incredible. That he should have heard from the lips of a stranger (for such Mrs. Leonard was to him at the time), who had never been inside his house, minute details about obscure books, and then to have all these details verified—the right book, the right page, the right part of the page, and the relevant message—well, it was too much of a strain on credulity! He tried to find passages equally appropriate, by chance, in a dozen books at the right and left of the designated book, but never found anything relevant in this manner.

The book tests seem to be highly evidential of intelligence beyond the grave. They are not, in themselves, conclusive—any more than the evidence from phantasms, mediumship, or automatisms was conclusive when taken alone. But, like these other phenomena, they are links in a chain of evidence which, when joined together, have a strength far beyond that possessed by each individually.

Beneath the tides of Sleep and Time
Strange fish are moving.
                    —Thomas Wolfe

6

THE TIME FRONTIER

ONE DAY WHEN MY YOUNGEST SON WAS ABOUT FIVE years old, he came to me with a question.

"Dad," he said, "what is 'tomorrow'?"

"Why, Wednesday," I replied.

"No, no!" he cried. "Not what *day* is it, but what *is* it?"

"Oh!" I said. "What *is* tomorrow? Well, it's the day after today."

His tiny brow furrowed in concentration. "But when it comes, it isn't tomorrow at all."

"No," I said, "when it comes, it's today."

"Then," he said, "tomorrow never really comes. It's always today."

There we left it for the time being, but for almost a year he continued to ask me questions that had to do with "today," "tomorrow," and "yesterday."

The colloquy about the days rang a bell somewhere in the back of my mind, and I recalled my old professor in Church History at Yale quoting something from St. Augustine: "Time!," the Bishop of Hippo observed, "what is it? If nobody asks me, I know. But if I am asked, I cannot describe it."

So my little son was in distinguished company in his ponderings on "The Eternal Now." He was grappling with a problem that has been the concern of the greatest minds of every age. Most men of necessity take time for granted. But the wiser members of the human race—philosophers, physicists, poets, and children—do not.

I said that most men take time for granted. That is an understatement. Most men, at least in the Western world, are time-obsessed. And this time-obsession, with its emphasis on deadlines, durations, and days of judgment, is responsible for a great deal of the misery that we find in the world. Time-obsession is the characteristic of all fanaticism; the time-obsessed religious faiths which believe in fast-approaching divine judgments and limited periods in which to redeem human souls from eternal punishment are the persecuting, proselytizing faiths. The Eastern religious groups and certain Western sects like the Quakers, whose emphasis is not on external events and prescribed doctrines but on the "inner light," do not persecute, do not proselytize. They know that time is relative and that God has no deadlines. It has been said that Isabella and Philip of Spain killed more people and caused more human suffering in obedience to conscience than Nero did in obedience to lust. This is entirely probable, and quite understandable. The Inquisition was running a race for souls against a divine Time-Keeper who held a quick stop-watch.

Time governs our lives. We chronicle its passing with calendars and clocks and dread the slow or quick approach of the last month, the last day, the last hour, the final tick that frees us from its domination. Yet—what is it? We do not know. Mathematically, it is a convenient abstraction, a humanly created device to regulate men and events and bring some sort of order into human relationships. And yet, as Immanuel Kant once said, we do not know that the "order" which time describes is the true order of the universe. Our conscious minds, the great German philosopher held, impose a certain order (spatio-temporal) on the events of the universe. This, he thought, might be due to the special pattern in which our sensory apparatus has evolved; the *true* order of the universe might be quite otherwise.

Obviously, this discussion of the nature of time is basic to any consideration of the survival of the human personality, or any part thereof, after what we call death. Death is our final capitulation to the time-abstraction; it is a "time" word, signifying a final halt in the world of time and space. But it can be shown that, abstraction or no, time is not the Absolute that we assume it is; that our view of it is not necessarily correct (that is, does not correspond to reality), and that there is a power of the mind or personality which pays no attention to our Absolute abstraction and is not subject to its limitations—then this evidence, coming on top of all the other evidence, must go a long way toward indicating the possibility, even the probability, of the survival of that mind or personality beyond the peremptory "halt" of death.

Man's preoccupation with the time problem goes back a long way in human history, although it was not until the emergence of modern science, about three hundred years ago, that time was defined as an Absolute, independent of all other human phenomena and subject to no modification or even analysis. The ancients were intrigued by time, but it was not an Absolute for them. They were very sure that on occasion the impenetrable veil could be pierced, even by the most ordinary of their own number. The Pythia at Delphi was always a woman, and generally one of the ignorant rural population. Yet, after fasting and inhaling the sacred vapors in the temple, she was believed to be capable of delivering messages from the gods and predicting future events. Oracles, augurs, soothsayers, Chaldeans, fortune-tellers, prophets—all were accepted and honored and their gifts taken quite as much as a matter of course as the gifts of the physician or the astronomer are today. A Nostradamus would not have caused undue excitement in the Babylon of Hammurabi; his capabilities would have been duly assessed and a suitable price put upon them. It would not have occurred to anyone that (because the time-barrier was absolute) a man could not have such powers and must thereby be a charlatan.

With the development of modern science, time was proclaimed an Absolute and prophecy fell into disrepute and illegality. For, if time was an Absolute, then no human being could violate its Absoluteness and predict a future event. Time was arbitrarily ruled an Absolute because such a hypothesis fitted the general world view which science was working out; it had not been *proved* an Absolute; indeed, the folklore and the psychic manifestations of several thousands of years of human history seemed to indicate that it was *not* an Absolute. But proclaiming it so freed science for intensive work on other problems. This proclamation limited science in much the same way that a leash limits a dog, but within the narrow confines of the leash science was able to sniff and explore thoroughly, to the benefit of all. Meanwhile, Elizabethan law took its lead from science and ordered the soothsayers who in ages past had enjoyed exalted status to be "taken adjudged and deemed rogues, vagabonds, and sturdy beggars."* Soon crusades against "witchcraft" were systematically stamping out every trace of extrasensory perceptivity, and mankind was well on its way to the present "sensate culture"

*39 Elizabeth c. 4 (1597), Sec. 2.

which Professor Pitirim A. Sorokin has analyzed so brilliantly. Here and there a philosopher like Kant, a mystic like Swedenborg, a psychologist like McDougall, or even a heretical scientist like Sir William Crookes sounded a note of dissent amidst the rising crescendo of scientific materialism; but generally speaking, time-tethered science was unchallenged in its best of all possible, three-dimensional worlds. Organized religion, almost as time-obsessed and time-tethered as science, did not seriously challenge the *Weltanschauung* of scientific materialism and indeed paid it the honor of trying desperately to bring its own creeds and dogmas within the beneficent radius of scientific approval. In this kind of a climate, prophecy was limited to the logical inference of the weather forecaster and the investment adviser; only the lowly racing fan with his illogical hunch could claim an unbroken relationship with the Pythia and Pilate's wife.

It remained for a scientist of impeccable reputation to drop a bombshell into the midst of this smug, three-dimensional world with its independent time-Absolute—Albert Einstein. In a period when only hair-shirted preachers, psychotic cultists, and science fiction writers were speculating about another dimension, Einstein calmly postulated his *space-time continuum,* with time as a fourth dimension. The Theory of Relativity added the alarm clock to the ruler as a measure of things, destroyed the independence of time as well as its Absoluteness, made it a coordinate of space, and opened up a whole new frontier for scientific research—the time frontier. Relativity cut the leash and permitted science to wander afield, although as yet it has not (except through the new science of parapsychology) gone very far away from the old stamping grounds.

Einstein and his Theory of Relativity caused a certain amount of public hilarity, but, as Professor A. N. Whitehead once observed, there is always an aspect of foolishness to really new ideas.* Comedians, columnists, and other jokesters had a lot of fun with Dr. Einstein and his incomprehensible talk about a space-time continuum, but scientists did not laugh. The space-time continuum, like Relativity itself, is now an accepted scientific dictum.

---

* *There was a young girl named Miss Bright,*
Who could travel much faster than light.
She departed one day
In an Einsteinian way,
And came back on the previous night.

The total effect of all this was not a definitive reply to the question, "What is tomorrow?"—that question, like the question of the nature of time itself, remains unanswered. It is no answer to say with Einstein that it is a fourth coordinate with the three spatial coordinates. It is that, but what *more* is it? That is like saying that an elephant is an animal with a long trunk—true enough, and worth knowing, but not by any means the whole truth.

What Einstein did was to shatter the untouchability of time as a scientific problem and bring it down from its lofty perch to where it could be examined. He made discussions of a fourth dimension (and perhaps other dimensions as well) intellectually respectable. And, as indicated, he paved the way for scientific research on the time frontier by severing the leash that limited the area of science's investigations. Science, because of his Theory of Relativity, is now free to tackle the problems of *time* as well as those of space, and to recognize the fact that the problems of space and time are related and may even turn out to be *one*. Einstein, indeed, holds that indubitably they *are* one, that space and time are only somewhat different aspects of the same basic reality.

Suffice it to say, then, that in exploring the time frontier we are now in good scientific company and do not automatically qualify for residence in the nearest mental institution.

Thomas Wolfe observed the strange fish that move beneath the tides of sleep and time. And the very best place to gain some insight into the real nature of time is in the phenomenon of sleep, or, more particularly, in dreams. The subconscious or subliminal mind knows nothing of the time abstraction that consciousness has devised; there is no "time" in dreams, and we dream of past, present, and (some hold) future with equal facility. A dream that encompasses days, months, and years of events may take place in a few minutes or even seconds of time. We have most of us had the experience of waking, looking at the clock, dozing off again and having a long, complicated dream that covers a considerable period of chronological time, only to wake again and discover that not more than two or three minutes have actually elapsed since last we looked at the clock. And it is a commonplace occurrence that in some moment of intense crisis—an accident, submersion, etc.—the events of a lifetime may flash in review before a consciousness shocked temporarily out of its subservience to the customary time abstraction.

The Society for Psychical Research, London, has compiled

extensive records on more than one thousand proven cases of precognition—that is, instances in which some future event has been previsioned (seen before it happened), often, but not always in dreams. These cases have been analyzed carefully to screen out occasions on which some kind of sensory perception may have been possible or some explicable function of the subconscious involved, such as the possibility that the person doing the previsioning may have subconsciously observed certain facts previously and drawn certain conclusions without being aware of it, the precognition then representing merely a form of subconscious inference that later turns out to be sound. Figuring out just when true previsioning takes place is admittedly a complicated business, but it has been done conscientiously by the psychologists and researchers of the London Society (people of the highest scientific integrity) and the result is a very impressive body of evidence, strongly suggestive of the existence of a power of the mind which is not limited by time. The following case, from the files of the Society, is a good illustration:

NARRATIVE STATEMENT OF DR. E. G. EAMES

On Saturday, May 24, 1930, I was driving as usual from St. Albans to London, along a road I knew exceedingly well, for I had traversed it hundreds and hundreds of times. My car is a fast one; I drive rapidly, for I am always in a hurry, and on this particular morning I had some five operations to perform in London before lunch.

But a preceding car prevented me from accelerating to a really quick speed. It was a Jowett, being driven carefully and quietly by a typical family man, in a typical leisurely manner, the father, mother, and kiddie all enjoying the run, one assumes.

In the ordinary way I should have passed by, as I pass by hundreds of similar tourists, and forgotten them. But on this occasion I absolutely could not pass. It was not the car that prevented me. On the contrary, it would have been easy to have got by, and I wanted to get by, but something insinuated the idea into my subconscious brain that an accident was going to occur. It was definitely a force quite apart from, shall I say, earthly impressions. It was in no way concerned with the driving of the man in front. Actually, he was driving very well. It certainly wasn't nerves. It was a very real presentiment that a crash was going to occur and a warning not to approach too near. For five miles I hesitated behind this slow-going old car, blaming my foolishness, but very much aware all the time of a holding back. Soon, however, I was to be very grateful indeed for this intimation, for when we reached a point in Watling Street between Radlet and St. Albans the looked-for accident occurred.

A lorry preceded the Jowett which was immediately in front of me, the three of us slowly making our ways to London. On the opposite side of the road, a saloon car had stopped. Suddenly the door of this stationary car opened; the huge lorry, obliterating the entire view of the road, could not quite get by. Without warning he stopped abruptly. The poor little Jowett went on. He turned out, found his road completely blocked in every direction, braked violently, skidded, and crashed first into the back part of the lorry and then into a brick wall.

And for five miles I had known very distinctly that it was going to happen, so very much so that during that time I had felt inclined to go up and mention my presentiment to the driver of the little family car.

All that remains to say is that being immediately behind I must in the ordinary way have been smashed up too, but had kept just far enough back to be able to come to a standstill immediately beside the wrecked car.

I attended to the little child, who was badly cut, and rushed both him and his mother to the Orthopaedic Hospital at Stanmore, where I left him in the hands of the surgeons.

A local police officer, reviewing all the details of the accident later, after measurements, etc. had been confirmed, was quite unable to understand at all how I had managed to avoid being injured or at least concerned in the smash, and when I rather reticently explained that I gathered something was going to happen, and this in spite of the care of the driver, he, knowing my usual speed, said: "It must have been a blooming strong *presentiment* for *you* to have waited behind."

This is the third time in my life that I have felt these strong compelling forces or influences warning me of danger, and always I have been afterwards very deeply grateful that I have been forewarned.*

Premonitions of the sort recounted here by Dr. Eames remind us that there are authenticated records of this sort of thing going back about as far in history as it is possible to go. Indeed, the Founder of Science himself, the very incarnation of sanity, shrewdness, and balance, was governed all his life by a monitory voice known as "The Daemon of Socrates." Plato gives us a good illustration of the functioning of this

---

Journal, Society for Psychical Research [London], Vol. XXVI [1915], p. 117.

"daemon" in his *Theages*. Timarchus is sitting at supper with
Socrates and rises to go out to a plot of assassination, to
which plot only one other man was privy:

> "What say you, Socrates?" said Timarchus. "Do you con-
> tinue drinking; I must go out somewhither, but will return in
> a little, if so I may." And the voice came to me; and I said
> to him, "By no means rise from the table; for the accustomed
> divine sign has come to me." And he stayed. And after a
> time again he got up to go, and said, "I must be gone, Socra-
> tes." And the sign came to me again; and again I made him
> stay. And the third time, determining that I should not see,
> he rose and said naught to me, when my mind was turned
> elsewhere; and thus he went forth, and was gone, and did
> that which was to be his doom.

To the end of his days, Socrates was guided by his "daemon." Call it a voice, a hunch, a trick of the subconscious or
what you will, the fact remains that Socrates was precogniz-
ing, was getting information about events before they happened. Moreover, not being bound by any scientific abstrac-
tions about time as an Absolute, he was not too surprised at
his gift.

The trance state, either hypnotic or mediumistic, is another
condition in which time as we know it has little meaning. On
one occasion the British medium Stella C. was being investigated by researchers working with the Society for Psychical
Research, London, and was in a deep trance when she suddenly stated that she could "see" the front page of the London *Daily Mail* as it would be thirty-seven days later—i.e.,
on May 19, 1923. She was able to give a very detailed description of the page, stating it contained a picture of a boy
falling down, white powder being poured out of a tin, a man
standing over the boy, and the name "Andrews Salt" in large
letters. The investigators took down all these details, sealed
the record, and filed it away. When the *Daily Mail* appeared
on Saturday, May 19, 1923, it carried on its front page a
full-ad for Andrews Liver Salts which was amazingly like the
one described by Stella C. while in trance. The researchers
got in touch with the manufacturers of the salts and the advertising manager of the *Daily Mail* to find out whether or
not the front page of the May 19 issue had been made up at
the time Stella C. "saw" it. These authorities agreed that a
rough sketch of the picture used in the ad had probably been
in existence, but that no exhibition of it had taken place and

that it had not been in anywhere the finished form in which the medium "saw" it while in trance. The newspaper editor added the information that the *Daily Mail* had not even decided to run the ad until April 28, something else having been tentatively scheduled for the space.

One of the most careful theoreticians about time was the late John W. Dunne. Dunne, who died recently, was a highly respected British aeronautical engineer whose theories about time have been incorporated in three fascinating, if somewhat complex, books, *Experiment with Time* (1927); *The Serial Universe* (1934); and *The New Immortality* (1938). Several of J. B. Priestley's best plays are based on Dunne's ideas.*

Dunne's interest in the time problem began with a series of odd premonitory dreams, the first of which occurred one night in 1898. Dunne dreamed that he was having an argument with a waiter in a restaurant over the time, the waiter insisting that it was half past four in the morning, while Dunne maintained that it was half past four in the afternoon. In his dream, Dunne concluded that his watch had stopped at four thirty and (still dreaming) he looked at his watch and saw that it had. Then he woke up. Remembering the odd dream, he reached for his watch, discovered that it was not at the bedside as it usually was, and finally located it on a chest of drawers. He looked at it and sure enough, it *had* stopped at exactly half past four. He concluded that it must have stopped the previous afternoon, and that he had taken note of this at the time but had forgotten it and remembered it in his dream. Then, still not knowing the right time, he rewound the watch but did not try to reset it. Later on in the morning when he arose for good, he checked the time and found that the watch was right within two or three minutes, or just about the time it would have taken him to wake up, find the watch and rewind it.

Some time later, while traveling in Italy, Dunne woke up one morning and wondered what time it was. His watch was not within reach, but, remembering his previous dream, he wondered if he could "see" the watch and discover the correct time without actually looking at it. He closed his eyes and lapsed into a sort of half-awake state. While in this semi-doze, he visualized the dial of the watch. The hour hand was on eight, and the minute hand wavered between twelve

---

*Dangerous Corner, 1932; Time and the Conways, 1937; I have been Here Before, 1937; Johnson Over Jordan, 1939.

and one. He decided to call it two and a half minutes past eight. Thereupon with some effort he roused himself and looked at the watch, and sure enough it was exactly two and a half minutes past eight.

There followed a whole series of premonitory dreams, all of which "came true," and Dunne, a sober man of science, became somewhat alarmed lest he be a victim of that defect of memory or recognition which psychologists call "identifying paramnesia." Equally disturbing was the possibility that he might be some kind of a psychic. These explanations, however, were discarded after a series of particularly vivid dreams of which the following is a good sample:

In his dream, Dunne was walking down a lane between two fenced fields. In one field was a horse which was rearing and pawing in a startling way, and Dunne looked to see if there was any way in which the beast could get out. However, there seemed to be no opening in the fence, so he walked on, reassured. But soon he heard the horse behind him, running madly down the lane. Dunne ran toward a flight of steps at the end of the lane, but woke up before he reached them.

The next day Dunne and his brother were fishing when the latter suddenly said: "Look at that horse!" Near the stream in which they were fishing was the exact setting of the previous night's dream—the fenced field, the lane, and even the steps at the end of the lane. And in the field was a frightened horse, nervously pawing the ground. Dunne thereupon began to recount his dream to his brother, but the horse began to act so oddly that he broke off the account to make sure the animal could not break through the fence. Having investigated the fence, he returned to his brother and said, "At any rate, *this* horse can't get out." A few minutes later, however, his brother cried, "Look out!" and sure enough, the horse had broken loose and was galloping down the path toward the steps, heading for the two men. It plunged into the stream, waded across, then turned away and ran off down the road.

After a series of dreams like the above, Dunne became convinced that he was neither a victim of identifying paramnesia nor a psychic, and he began a process of intricate theorizing which led him finally to the ideas about time which are outlined in his books. The dreams he had had, he decided, were just ordinary dreams, but they were misplaced in time. Instead of coming *after* the event, they were coming *before* it. The dreams themselves were all right, but he was having them on the *wrong nights!* His dream about the horse, for instance, was the kind of a dream one might normally expect *after* having seen the horse break out and galloping down the lane. But he had had it *before* observing the strange actions of the animal.

Conversation with friends and others disclosed that many of them, too, had had similar wrong-time dreams, but had either forgotten them or dismissed them as mere oddities. Dunne became convinced that many such dreams occurred, but were unnoticed because the dream was not sharp enough or because the dreamer failed to notice the relationship between the dream and the subsequent event. He decided that all dreams were made up of images of past experience and images of future experience blended together in equal proportions, and that the universe is really *stretched out* in time. The conventional view in which the future is cut off from the present and past is due to a purely mentally imposed barrier which exists only in the conscious mind; that is to say, only when we are awake. The associational network stretches not merely this way and that in space, but also backwards and forwards in time; in dreams we continually cross and recross that nonexistent equator which, when awake, we rule arbitrarily athwart the whole. Just as our dream-consciousness ignores the limitations of space, going in a second from one scene to another many miles away, so it also ignores the limitations of time. Dunne went on from here to develop his theory of "serialism," which holds that reality as it appears to human science has to be a series of regresses reaching back into infinity. Dunne's theories, dealing as they do with quanta, wave effects, Uncertainty Principles, and regresses are somewhat complicated for the layman, but they are taken seriously (even if not generally accepted) by physicists. What they add up to is Dunne's belief that the time barrier is really nonexistent and is merely the creature of consciousness, and that there is a common faculty of the subconsciousness which pays no attention to the alleged barrier.

Dunne's theories seem to receive some striking confirmation in precognition's sister phenomenon, retrocognition, or what the French call *déjà-vue*—the feeling of "having been there before."

Most of us have had at some time or other the sensation of odd familiarity with a new place. Psychologists have usually explained such cases on the grounds of paramnesia or some other disturbance of memory, and undoubtedly many of them do fall in this category. However, there are also a large number of carefully documented cases which clearly come outside of the disturbance-of-memory classification, and if we can accept precognition as a fact there is little to keep us from also accepting retrocognition. If the mind is not limited in its progress forward in time, it can hardly be limited in its backward reach into the distant past. Moreover, the laboratory tests at Duke University and at the University of London have apparently established retrocognition experimentally quite as firmly as they have established precognition. However, the evidence here is admittedly not as clear as it is for precognition, for the simple reason that everything that lies in the past is a matter of record somewhere, or was at some time, and so there are possible alternative explanations to true retrocognition if one accepts the reality of such subliminal powers as telepathy and clairvoyance. But let us look at one or two intriguing cases of apparent retrocognition.

The first case is described by Lady Radnor, who was present with Miss A. Goodrich Freer in Salisbury Cathedral, England, when it happened. Both of these ladies were of excellent reputation and standing, and Miss Freer was one of those upper-class, amateur mediums whom we find so often in the history of psychical research, and who are not to be confused with the professional, money-seeking mediums of ill-repute.

On February 23, 1890, Miss A. and I were in the "Cage" (Hungerford Chapel of Salisbury Cathedral) when she told me that she suddenly "saw" a grand ceremonial taking place. There appeared to be a tall chair which obstructed the view down the choir, and gradually the place appeared with clericals and others dressed in their best attire. Then she "saw" a tall, big man, slowly walking up, dressed in red and with white lace over it, something that hung around his neck and down to his feet of gold and embroidery, and a broad sort of mitre (but not peaked) more like a biretta, of beautiful embroidery.

Then there were three or four dressed very much like him, gorgeously dressed, and lots of little boys about in red and white and lace—holding candles, books, etc. The whole place was very full of people, and it was evidently a great occasion. After the principal figure had knelt in front of the chair—looking to the west for some little time—he stood up, and ten little boys lifted up the chair, and carried it higher up and placed it in front of the altar, still facing west. Then the principal figure walked up two steps and faced the east. (The whole of the arrangements of the altar, etc. as Miss A. "saw" them, are quite different from what they are now, and were later identified by Lord Radnor as being quite correct for their time.) He had nothing on his head now. He knelt some little time, and then the most gorgeously dressed of the other figures placed something like a mitre on his head and retired, and the principal figure walked up to the chair, and sat down on it facing the congregation. Miss A. said she "saw" him later dead in a coffin, with the Winchester Cross over him. She said he was tall, big, clean-shaven, with curling hair and blue-gray eyes.

Miss A. "asked" what it was that she was "seeing" and the "answer" came faintly to her:

"The induction of Briant Uppa."

Then Miss A. said: "There can't be such a name; it must be wrong."

(A) "You are wrong. It is Duppa, not Uppa. Brian Duppa."

Question by Miss A.: "Who was Brian Duppa?"

(A) "Chister."

(Q) "What was he?"

(A) "Bishop here."

(Q) "When? What was his date?"

(A) "44-16. His researches should help you. Manuscripts should lay in Winchester."

On returning home we were talking after tea, and I casually took up Britton's *History of Wiltshire,* and said to Miss A., laughing: "Now I will look for your bishop." The pages where the bishops were named were uncut, sides and top. I cut them, and to our delight we found on page 149:

"Brian Duppa or De Uphaugh, D.D. . . . tutor to Prince Charles . . . translated to the See of Chichester (Chister) . . . Bishop of 1647 . . . deposed soon after by Parliament . . . preferred soon after the Restoration to the See of Winchester."

We further discovered that Brian Duppa was at Carisbrooke with Charles I, and is supposed to have assisted him in the writing of the *Eikon Basilike,* which book Miss A. had been looking at in my boudoir a few days previously, but which contains no mention of him nor his name.*

Whatever the explanation, this is a curious case. Had Miss A.'s mind suddenly leaped the time barrier on that February afternoon in the old cathedral (where all the conditions were ripe for such a phenomenon) and skipped back through the

* Entire account in F. W. H. Myers, *Human Personality,* pp. 592-93.

centuries to pick up a colorful event that had once taken
place there? Or had she read all about the induction of Brian
Duppa sometime in the dim past and then forgotten it until
external circumstances brought it powerfully to mind? Or had
she simply faked the whole thing?

Conventional psychology, of course, would prefer either of
the latter two explanations, but there are very excellent reasons
why neither of these is satisfactory. The first is not satisfactory
because Miss A. (like Dunne) had had many similar
experiences and had insofar as she knew never heard of
Brian Duppa until that February afternoon. The second falls
short because Miss A. had a splendid reputation, was an intimate
of people like Frederic W. H. Myers, and, being an amateur,
had no motive for fraud. Parapsychology would insist
that the first explanation (true retrocognition) deserves to be
taken seriously.

One of the most intriguing (and controversial) instances of
alleged retrocognition is the one described in a little book
called *An Adventure*, which was first published in 1911 and
has been republished as recently as 1947.* The book was
written by two estimable English ladies who were also distinguished
scholars, C. Anne E. Moberly, principal of St.
Hugh's College, Oxford; and a member of her staff who later
succeeded her as principal at St. Hugh's, Eleanor F. Jourdain.

The two Englishwomen, traveling in France, had visited
the Petit Trianon at Versailles in August, 1901. The Petit
Trianon, however, was somehow different from what they
had expected; the air was still and oppressive, and both
women later confessed that without saying anything about it
to the other, each had felt like screaming with nervousness.
Neither, it should be added, was normally in the least hysterical
or distraught. Oddly enough, on this particular hot summer
day there were no other tourists about. The buildings did
not seem to be in the places where current maps said they
should be, and some were not on the maps at all. Odd, uncharted
paths appeared; the gardeners and others whom they
encountered were dressed in the clothes of another era and
spoke a French much older than that currently in vogue in
Paris. They saw strange people, and heard strange noises. A
pretty woman, dressed in a long-outmoded cape, sketched in
a garden, and an evil-looking man with a pock-marked face

---

*Moberly and Jourdain, *An Adventure* [London: The Macmillan Co.,
1911].

followed them about. In the distance a band played, although
there was no band in evidence anywhere. Everything was
odd, eerie, and old, and the two teachers finally retired from
the Petit Trianon, baffled but relieved to be out of the strange
atmosphere.

Later on they returned to the Petit Trianon and discovered
it to be quite different from what it had appeared to be on
their first visit. There were crowds of tourists about; gardeners, attendants, and gendarmes were dressed as they should
be; and everything was in its right place. The Petit Trianon
they had seen the first time had completely disappeared.

There then began for the two Englishwomen a long process of comparing old maps, documents, and fashion books,
and an exhaustive correspondence with French historians and
other authorities. These researchers finally convinced the ladies that the Petit Trianon they had "seen" on the occasion of
their first visit was not the current Petit Trianon but the Petit
Trianon as it had been in the time of Marie Antoi-
nette—1789. The documents they offered in substantiation
of their theory were taken seriously enough to be accepted by
the Bodleian Library. These documents have been carefully
studied by psychologists and psychical researchers, who
promptly split on their significance, some holding that the ladies had indubitably "visited" the Petit Trianon as it was in
1789, while others insisted that there was some more normal
explanation for what happened. The London Society for
Psychical Research was at first highly skeptical, but later
modified its skepticism somewhat.

Maurice Maeterlinck, the playwright and author who
maintained a lifelong interest in the problem of time, had an
interesting theory. In his little-known volume, *The Life of
Space,* he comments on the fact that the star Mira, in the
constellation of Balaena the Whale, is seventy-two light years
away from our earth. Suppose, he says, there is on Mira a
civilization more advanced than ours, and an astronomer
with a telescope or some more perfect apparatus (a super-
television would do nicely, but Maeterlinck didn't know
about that) powerful enough to distinguish clearly what is
going on on earth. What the Mira astronomer would see
through his apparatus would not be Paris, London, or New
York as they are today *to us,* but those cities as they were
seventy-two years ago, horse-cars in the streets, bustles on the
ladies, and all the rest. There would be no trace of two world
wars, for they would not yet have happened as far as the as-

tronomer on Mira was concerned—the present, for him, is that which he sees. For him, the immobile and subterranean life of the past *is* the present; the crowds which pass before his eyes on Fifth Avenue and the Boulevard St. Germain have not risen from their tombs, for they have not yet entered them. Which "time" is right? Maeterlinck concludes: "In this plurality of times which are merely pure conventions, are not the events of the future already present somewhere, just as the events of the past are still present? They cannot be stinted for room, since the present is eternal, which means that it is infinite in space as well as in time."*

J. W. Dunne's theory of serialism, or infinite regress, as an explanation for precognition and retrocognition has already been mentioned. Still another interesting theory is that of Dr. C. D. Broad, an English scientist, who holds to the possibility that there may be a *second dimension of time,* which normally we know nothing about, lying at right angles to our familiar dimension. Says Professor Broad:

If there is only one temporal dimension, any two events of finite duration are either separated by a temporal gap or are adjoined, so that the end of one exactly coincides with the beginning of the other or they wholly or partially overlap. But if there be a second temporal dimension, events which are separated by a temporal gap in one dimension may be adjoined without any gap in the other, just as two points in the earth's surface which differ in longitude may be identical in latitude."†

For instance, says Professor Broad, we may imagine our familiar "time" as being represented by a line going from west to east, and the second (or unknown) dimension by a line going from south to north. To illustrate—Mother Shipton, who lived in the sixteenth century, is alleged to have foretold the invention of automobiles. The two-dimensional time theory would explain this by saying that although in our familiar dimension of time, the invention of the automobile occurred more than two centuries *after* Mother Shipton's prediction, yet, in the second (south-north) dimension of time, it

*Maurice Maeterlinck, *The Life of Space* [New York: Dodd, Mead & Co., 1928].

†From a paper entitled "The Philosophical Implications of Foreknowledge," read by Professor Broad to the Aristotelian Society and Mind Association, London, July, 1937.

occurred just *before* the prediction. In other words, what she was doing actually was *remembering*, not predicting.

A third theory about time is called the *Theory of the Greater Specious Present*, and is put forward by Mr. H. F. Saltmarsh of the Society for Psychical Research, London.* It is based on the conception, generally accepted in psychology, that the "present moment" in which we act is not a mere point-instant, but occupies a definite period of duration. Within this "specious present" there is no present, past, or future, but rather a gradation with respect to clearness of apprehension of whatever lies within its compass, maximum clearness being at the center.

Now, consciousness is often likened to a rock standing in water, or to an iceberg. Only a small part of it—perhaps a tenth—is above water. This is the normal consciousness. The nine-tenths of the rock or iceberg lying beneath the surface of the water is the subconsciousness, or the subliminal. So far as the normal, conscious mind is concerned, this specious present is of short duration, but the subliminal consciousness, beneath the surface, may broaden out and have a much greater span. Thus, some events which are past or future as far as the limited specious present of normal consciousness is concerned, might still be present to the much broader subconsciousness with its wider specious present. What this boils down to, of course, is an argument that time is a reality only for the conscious mind.

One question that immediately arises when we examine this intriguing problem of precognition is this: is everything then predestined, and does man have no free will at all? Saltmarsh answers this by saying that man does indeed have a measure of free will. He likens the world to a series of parallel wires seen through a slot, which moves in the direction of their length. All the wires are rigidly frozen in the past, the region over which the slot has already passed, and some of them are also frozen in the future—the area which the moving slot has not yet reached. Some of the wires, however, can be reached through the slot by the human percipient and manipulated by him, and this movement extends through the whole of their future length. This is the extent of man's "free will." However, it gives man a considerable area of volition and permits him to modify circumstances that might other-

---

*See his "Report on Cases of Apparent Precognition," *Proceedings of the Society for Psychical Research* [London], Vol. XLII [1932], p. 49 ff.

wise lead to inevitable discomfiture or doom. Thus, the broad, specious present of the subconsciousness may become aware of a disastrous event, knowledge of which has not yet reached the narrower, specious present of the normal consciousness, and may flash danger signals into the normal consciousness, via troublesome dreams or otherwise, that will if heeded enable the normal consciousness to avoid the disaster: e.g., to manipulate the wires and change "destiny."

All of these theories, of course, are subject to considerable criticism, and the criticisms are even more complex and unintelligible to the layman than the theories themselves. And heaven knows these latter are difficult enough! They are cited here not as representing working hypotheses of science in pioneering on this new "time frontier," but as a preliminary scouting of the terrain that has been carried on by some of the more adventuresome in science, philosophy, and psychology.

This, then, is the raw material with which we must deal and from which we must attempt to assay the truth about time. It looks promising; it intrigues us; here and there we see a glint of pure gold. Is there a power of the mind, or personality, or subconsciousness (call it what you will) that is not limited by time, and that therefore may logically be expected to survive that time-halt that we call death? The raw material cited here, and the theories of Dunne, Broad, Saltmarsh, and even Einstein, seem to indicate that there is.

But "indicate" is not enough. Is there laboratory *proof* of such a power of the mind? Can that power be tested and proved experimentally, and with the utmost scientific rigor?

Let us see.

7

MIND UNDER
THE MICROSCOPE

UP UNTIL 1930, PSYCHICAL RESEARCH, IN SPITE OF ALL ITS accomplishments and its devotion to the scientific method, could not call itself a branch of science. The eminent physicists, biologists, astronomers, philosophers, and scholars who had affiliated with the American and English Societies for Psychical Research were certainly men of science, but most of them were careful to maintain a distinction between themselves as individuals and their various professional fields. The prevailing materialism of science as a whole forced this stratagem upon them. As individuals they could engage in psychical research as a hobby, but they could not associate themselves professionally—as chemists, physicists, biologists, etc.—with it. However, the examination of mediumship, the study of the cross-correspondences and book tests, the analysis of "phantasms," etc. all were carried on with the utmost scientific rigor and it is that which gives them the high evidential value they have. William James, as a psychologist, could not identify psychology with his study of Mrs. Piper, but his work with her and his final conclusions about her do put a stamp of intellectual approval on her work that it would not otherwise possess.

Until 1930, the men of science in psychical research recognized clearly that the scientific climate was too hostile to make feasible the establishment of the study of psychical phenomena as a recognized and accepted branch of science. So, while they examined carefully the evidence that had been accumulating through the ages—the folk tales, the hauntings, the poltergeists, the miraculous healings, and all the rest—they refrained from doing that which is the very essence of the scientific method—the devising of controlled and repeata-

ble laboratory experiments. They had the *hypotheses* and the
hypotheses had been unofficially verified by psychical research. But they did not translate the hypotheses into the kind
of laboratory experiments which could transform psychical research from the status of hobby to a science. In the first place,
they felt that the cards were stacked against them by their fellow scientists, and, in the second place, the setting up of laboratories and equipment costs money.

The scientific climate, however, was undergoing some
changes. The development of psychology as a "science of the
soul" had effected a modification of the stark materialism of
nineteenth century science. Such psychologist-philosophers as
William James, William McDougall, Henri Bergson, and Hans
Driesch had upheld the dual (physical-spiritual) nature of
man and had preached a *personalistic* philosophy that was in
striking contrast to the *behaviorism* (materialism) of the John
B. Watson school. Sigmund Freud had shown that mind and
body can be healed through the mind, and his excavation of
the subconscious had dealt a hard blow to the materialists.
Freud himself was certainly no religionist, but the total effect
of his work was to discredit that branch of psychology which
depended on the syringe, the scalpel, and electrical apparatus
to understand the mind of man.

Thus, in spite of the furious controversies between behaviorists and non-behaviorists that raged within it, the establishment of psychology as a respected branch of science prepared
the way for the coming of psychical research into the scientific family. Psychology was, by definition, concerned with
the soul, the "psyche," the non-material element in human
personality, and so was psychical research. There were many
to scoff at the latter and to fight its acceptance as a science,
just as there had been many to scoff at and to fight the acceptance of psychology itself, but in the end the scientific
spirit *per se* demanded its acceptance. And so psychical research rode into the camp of science on the coattails of
psychology, and when it got there it changed its name to "parapsychology" (a study of phenomena that are beyond the
present scope of psychology).

Today parapsychology *is* an accepted member of the scientific family, even though some of the members of the family
view it with amusement and others with distaste. But science
as a whole accepts parapsychology as a serious and legitimate
study and increasingly looks to it for guidance in the endless
scientific search for an answer to the question the Psalmist

once asked: "What is man?" Four great universities now grant doctorates for research in the field of parapsychology, and there are parapsychology societies in Washington and at Harvard. One of the moving figures in the latter group is the famous sociologist Pitirim A. Sorokin. At Duke and Harvard universities and the City College of New York in this country, and at London and Cambridge in England, work in the field of parapsychology is going on all the time. The new science has its own professional organ, *The Journal of Parapsychology,* which is edited by the distinguished American parapsychologist, Joseph B. Rhine. As "parapsychology," psychical research has at last attained scientific respectability.

The link between psychical research as the hobby of some respected intellectuals and parapsychology as an accepted branch of science is Dr. William McDougall. Professor McDougall, who was perhaps the most universally respected of all modern psychologists, came from Oxford University to head the Department of Psychology at Harvard in 1920. There he became the leader of the purposive psychologists in their struggle with Watson's "behaviorists." He also insisted that phsycical research should become a university study —i.e., a science.* Finding a sum of money available at Harvard for this purpose, he promptly began to practice what he was preaching by putting two of his brightest graduate students to work doing psychical research. One of them was Dr. Gardner Murphy, who is today one of the country's outstanding psychologists and a leading protagonist of parapsychology at the City College of New York.

McDougall's insistence that psychical research ought to be a university study attracted the attention of Joseph and Louisa Rhine, two young biologists at the University of Chicago. Rhine had gone to college to study for the ministry, but his studies had shown him the apparent lack of scientific basis for many of the tenets of his religious faith, and he had turned to biology. The materialism of biology, however, was even more depressing than the lack of scientific undergirding for religion. When Rhine and his wife read McDougall's writings, they decided that these writings seemed to point to the kind of science for which they were looking. So, in 1926, they came on from Chicago to take graduate work in psychology with McDougall at Harvard. In 1927, when McDougall left

*See McDougall's essay on "Psychical Research as a University Study" in *The Psychic Source-Book,* pp. 28-44.

Harvard to head the Department of Psychology at Duke, the Rhines went with him. McDougall said of Rhine that he was "a ruthless seeker after truth . . . a whole-hearted scientist for whom philosophy and theology are but pre-skirmishes beyond the frontiers of scientific knowledge." In 1928 Rhine became a member of the faculty at Duke, under McDougall, and in 1931, they together set up the world's first official Laboratory of Parapsychology at Duke. With its establishment, the way was now open for the creation of controlled experiments and the testing of what Rhine called "extra-sensory perception" under laboratory conditions.

The first thing that the new science had to prove experimentally in the laboratory was the actual existence of a non-material element, a "psi capacity" (short for psychic) in life. That was the first step toward proving (if it could be proved) that there was an element in man (a "soul," if you like) that could survive the universal experience of death. To Spiritualists, Theosophists, orthodox Christians, and religionists of every stripe, as well as to many veteran psychical researchers, this was pettifogging. They had long since established the existence of a spiritual element in life, at least to their own satisfaction, and the insistence of parapsychology on going back to the very beginning and proving it all over again seemed like foolishness and a waste of time to them. What they overlooked was the fact that they had not arrived at their conclusions about the spiritual component in life via the scientific method, and that only an answer to life's questions arrived at by that method would satisfy science. And, such was the authority of science, only an answer that satisfied science would gain that general acceptance on which action is based. In other words, people might give lip service to the idea of immortality because philosophers, theologians, mediums, and psychical researchers assured them it was true, but they would not *live* as though it were true until *science* told them so.

The laboratory job, as Rhine and McDougall saw it, was to determine whether or not there was a spiritual component in life and, if there was, to demonstrate it in simple, easily controlled experiments that could be repeated on demand. The experiments would have to be based on mathematics—a universal science which was exact and about which there could be no dispute. They would have to employ devices which lent themselves readily to statistical analysis, and the analysis would have to be done, not by parapsychologists, but by trained and impersonal statisticians. To this end, the laboratory at Duke enlisted the services of a mathematician, Dr. J. A. Greenwood. Later, the American Institute of Mathematical Statistics, after a careful study of the mathematics involved in the Duke tests, issued the following statement:

> Dr. Rhine's investigations have two aspects, experimental and statistical. On the experimental side, mathematicians of course have nothing to say. On the statistical side, however, recent mathematical work has established the fact that, assuming that the experiments have been properly performed, the statistical analysis is essentially valid. If the Rhine investigation is to be fairly attacked, it must be on other than mathematical grounds.

By now, Dr. Rhine's books, *New Frontiers of the Mind* and *The Reach of the Mind,* have made the first experiments at Duke, involving cards and dice, fairly well known. The original storm stirred up by the announcement of these tests has somewhat died down now, so it may be worthwhile to look briefly at them before going on to the more complicated experiments which have more direct bearing on the problem of survival.

The first experiments were designed to prove (or disprove) simple clairvoyance—the ability of the mind to perceive truth without employing sensory perception. This was a sort of a seeing with the mind's eye rather than with the physical eye. For these tests a special deck of cards was devised, called ESP (for extra-sensory perception) cards. There were five suits of five cards each, the suits being designated by symbols: a cross, a wavy line, a star, a square, and a circle. The idea, in the simplest test, was for the subject to tell what the symbol on the face of the card was without looking at it. He could simply close his eyes and call out the order of the deck as he "saw" it in his mind, or he might look at the *back* of the cards. (Later, subjects could not look at the backs of the cards, as the tests were criticized on the grounds that subjects with especially keen eyesight might see *through* them, or that imperfections in manufacture might enable the subject to associate certain imperfections with certain symbols.) Sometimes the tests combined *telepathy* with clairvoyance, with an agent looking at the card and then trying to convey the right symbol *telepathically* to the subject.*

*Anyone wishing to purchase these cards may do so by writing to the Institute of Parapsychology, F.R.N.M, College Station, Durham, N.C. 27708.

The whole thing is based on the mathematics of *chance*—the same principle that insurance companies use in setting their rates. From chance alone, the subject could expect to make 5 correct card calls out of 25 cards. Odds of 100 to 1 are generally accepted in science as ruling out chance, but at Duke the parapsychologists set the ratio at 500 to 1. Anything less than that would not be accepted as significant.

Now—if a subject went through the deck four times (calling 100 cards) and scored an average of 7.5 hits per run (total of 30 hits), the odds, according to mathematics, would be 150 to 1 against such a score occurring by chance alone. That, in the eyes of the parapsychologists, would not be significant. But if a subject (and one did) went through the deck just once and called the first nine cards correctly, the odds against that being due to chance would be five raised to the ninth power (5^9) against 1! Very significant, indeed, even to a parapsychologist.

During the first three years at Duke, various subjects made a total of 3,400 runs through the deck of ESP cards in the telepathy-clairvoyance tests—the simplest tests to indicate whether there actually *was* a "mind's eye," or "non-material element" in life—calling 85,000 separate cards. The general average for all of these "calls" was 7 hits per 25 calls. This was an average of two above chance per run. As we have seen, an average of 7.5 hits per run for four runs gives odds of 150 to 1 against chance being responsible. The odds against an average of 7 hits per run being maintained for 3,400 runs is so astronomical that the figures would cross this page and spill over onto the next! Even a small average above chance—say 5.75—is statistically very significant if it is maintained for a large number of runs.

Remember, these tests were all carried out under laboratory conditions. There was nothing hit or miss about them. They were supervised by trained scientists and analyzed by professional mathematicians. Extraordinary precautions were taken to prevent any sensory perception from taking place. Mechanical card-shufflers were used; opaque screens were erected between the experimenter and the subject; the cards themselves were often enclosed in envelopes; elaborate systems of deck-cutting were employed.

Under these circumstances, some of the results attained were truly amazing. One subject called nine cards in a row correctly, and on another occasion, the same subject called fifteen in a row without error. The odds against that being due to chance are 30,000,000,000 to 1! Another subject averaged nine hits per run, with the cards which he was calling in a building 100 yards away from him. According to the laws of physics, the extension of the distance between the subject and the cards from one yard to 100 yards should have resulted in a decrease in his scoring rate to 1/10,000 of what it was at one yard. Obviously some other law than the law of physics was operating here. A little Negro girl, having been promised some candy if she made a good score, closed her eyes and *called every card correctly!* A graduate student in the laboratory performed the same feat.

After hundreds of thousands of these tests had been made and analyzed statistically, Dr. Rhine and his colleagues (McDougall had since retired) were justified in claiming that the existence of a "psi capacity," a non-material component in life, had been scientifically proved.

The attention at Duke then turned to another field—psychokinesis. Could this psi capacity, the extra-sensory non-material element, be used to affect material objects? In other words, could the mind produce a spiritual, a mental, form of energy, that could be *measured?*

In the psychokinesis experiment, dice were used. Could the mind influence the fall of the dice? Gamblers from the beginning of time had been very sure that it could, but science had not concerned itself with such "nonsense."

The typical PK (for psycho-kinesis) test was as simple as the ESP tests with the cards had been. The subject chose a target number, say six, and then tried to *will* the dice to fall in some combination that added up to six. Twelve throws of the dice constituted a "run," and two sixes out of twelve thrown could be expected from chance alone. The same elaborate precautions were taken to prevent any sensory influence on the dice—they were specially made, were thrown from a special cup, and, finally, mechanical dice throwers were employed.

The first nine hundred runs of the dice produced an average of only .50 above chance. However, this meant a total of 446 hits above chance for the whole run of 900. The odds against this happening by chance is a number represented by 20 digits to 1.

So PK, too, would seem to have been established as a fact.

Duke University was not the only place where scientific experiments bearing on telepathy, clairvoyance, and psychokinesis were being carried on. Professor H. J. F. W. Brugmans and G. Heymans at the University of Groningen, in the Netherlands, carried out a highly successful series of experiments involving the identification of blocks. Two young instructors at the University of Colorado carried out a series of experiments using regular playing cards. At Hunter College in New York, Professor Bernard Riess supervised 1,850 trials with the Duke ESP cards, and discovered that one of his students had averaged eighteen hits per run with a distance of one quarter mile intervening between subject and agent. At the City College of New York, Dr. Gertrude Schmeidler carried on an interesting series of experiments to determine whether or not belief or disbelief in the possibility of paranormal cognition had any effect on the scoring. (It did!) At the University of London, in England, Professor S. G. Soal, the mathematician, engaged in a long series of experiments involving *precognitive telepathy* (about which more later).

Outside of the universities, many well-known individuals were engaged in experiments of one sort or another. Among the experimenters were the French engineer René Warcollier, the German doctor Carl Bruck, the German scientist Rudolph Tischner, the British explorer Sir Hubert Wilkins, and the American author Upton Sinclair. Both Professor McDougall and Albert Einstein appealed for a scientific hearing for the book which Sinclair wrote describing his experiments with telepathy. All of these men, no less than the parapsychologists at Duke, affirmed that there *was* a spiritual component in life (a soul) and that it could be demonstrated statistically. The first task of the new science of parapsychology was accomplished. It had demonstrated, experimentally, the existence of a non-material element; an element that was independent of brain cells, nervous systems, and body chemistry. It had proved, moreover, that this non-material element was capable of exerting *energy* against material objects.

Now we come to the matter that is of most interest to us in this study. The laboratory experiments had shown that *distance* was no barrier to the functioning of this extra-sensory ability. If *distance* (space) was not a barrier, was it conceivable that *time* also was not a barrier? Had not Einstein shown that time and space were but opposite sides of a coin, and had not science accepted what it called the "space-time continuum"? In other words, could *precognition,* or prophecy, and *retrocognition,* the sense of "I-have-been-here-before," be demonstrated experimentally as telepathy, clairvoyance, and psychokinesis had been demonstrated? If so, a tremendous hurdle to a belief in the survival of the human personality after death would be cleared.

What was the simplest test that could be devised for finding out whether or not this spiritual component in life was subject to the limitation of *time?* At Duke, it was decided that the same deck of cards which had been used to test telepathy and clairvoyance could also be used to test *precognition.* In 1933, a subject by the name of H.P. was asked to try to predict the order of the pack of cards *as it would be after it was shuffled!*

H.P. followed this procedure: he wrote down the 25 symbols in the order in which he thought they would be at the conclusion of the experiment. After this he cut the cards five times. Then he *shuffled* the deck. Finally, he checked the order of the cards against his prediction of what the order would be.

H.P. scored an average of 7.1 hits per run of 25. Chance, of course, would account for only 5 hits per run.

Five other subjects then began a long series of similar tests for precognition. In 1,206 runs, they averaged 5.8 hits per 25, which gives a CR (critical ratio) of 12.0. The 1,452 total runs for all six subjects averaged 6.0 per run, 1.0 above chance, with a CR of 19.3.

Between 1934 and 1937, a total of 113,075 separate card calls were made to test precognition. They were given in fifteen series to a total of forty-nine subjects, and resulted in an average of 5.14 hits per 25. This did not seem to be much, but when it was maintained over such a long series, it gave a deviation of 614 above the mean chance expectation of 22,615. Mathematically speaking, this gave a critical ratio of 4.5—or odds of more than 400,000 to 1 that such deviation would occur by chance alone. The chance hypothesis was, therefore, excluded.*

In England, experiments of a different order were taking place. Originally designed to test clairvoyance, they showed evidence not only of clairvoyance, but also of something which the parapsychologists called *displacement.*

These experiments were carried out by Mr. Whately Car-

*For a full account of these experiments, see J. B. Rhine, "Experiments Bearing on the Precognition Hypothesis: Pre-Shuffling Card Calling," *Journal of Parapsychology* [Durham, N. C.: Duke University], Vol. II [1938].

ington of Cambridge University. On ten successive evenings
he chose an object at random and pinned up a drawing of it
on a curtain in his study. He had previously arranged with
people in England, Holland, and the United States simulta-
neously (making proper allowance for the difference in time,
of course) to try to "get" the object by clairvoyance and
draw a picture of it as they saw it with the mind's eye. Ten
evenings in a row made up a series. After several series, Carington's friends sent their drawings in to him at Cambridge.
Carington then had them judged by an authority who was
kept in ignorance as to exactly which drawing had been ex-
hibited on any particular evening. He scored 1 for a good
likeness, ½ for a likeness good in some respects, and 0 for a
drawing that was totally unlike the target.

As far as clairvoyance was concerned, this series of tests
was inconclusive. But the judging authority and Carington
both noted an odd phenomenon—the drawings for a given
series resembled much more closely the targets used for that
series than they did the ten targets used in any other series.
For instance, if a bowl of fruit was the target for Tuesday,
there was a definite tendency for the drawers to draw bowls
of fruit on Monday or Wednesday nights, and a much smaller
tendency to draw bowls of fruit on Thursday, Friday, or Saturday nights. This seemed to indicate that the drawers on any
given evening were often getting mind-pictures of targets that
were going to be pinned up one or two evenings later or had
been pinned up the previous evening. This *displacement in
time* seemed on the face of it to bear out J. W. Dunne's theories about time and strongly indicated some power of *previsioning* or precognition on the part of at least some of the
drawers.

Previous to this, Dr. S. G. Soal of the University of London had conducted a long series of card tests similar to the
ones carried out at Duke. He had supervised 128,000 card-
guessing trials and had been somewhat discouraged when the
results were no better than what could have been expected
from chance. However, after reading about Carington's dis-
covery of the *displacement in time* phenomenon in his picture tests, Soal went carefully back over the results of his
own tests, this time looking for evidence of displacement. He
discovered that 2 of his 160 experimenters *had* been scoring
significantly on the cards one or two places ahead or behind
the target card.

The better of the two was a man by the name of Basil

Shackleton. A special experiment was worked out for him
with a series of cards bearing the pictures of five different animals. The agent would look at the card and Shackleton
would try to tell what it was, getting the information telepathically from the mind of the agent. In this series of experiments, the results showed conclusively that Shackleton was
perceiving the mental picture of the animal, not as it *was,* but
as it *would be* in approximately three seconds' time! This displacement was so consistent and so marked that Soal and
other parapsychologists who studied the experiment were
convinced that Shackleton was indeed *previsioning* the cards,
and that here was positive experimental proof that such previsioning was possible. Later experiments with other subjects
convinced Soal that displacement *backward* in time as well as
forward was possible, thus bearing out the hypothesis that *retrocognition* as well as precognition is possible.

Now, it is difficult for us to fully comprehend the significance of all these experiments. Statistics are dry things and it
is hard to clothe them with life. They are impersonal; they
lack the dramatic impact of the appearance of a phantasm or
the intellectual challenge of a psychic puzzle like the cross-
correspondences or the book tests. Yet their very dryness and
impersonality are the keys to their great significance. Here is
evidence divorced from human imagination. It is objective,
cold and analyzable. And, if the mathematics of it be correct,
it is unchallengeable. It is, in other words, proof—scientific,
laboratory proof.

If this is hard reading, if you can't get excited over it, if it
bores you—well, I expect that Galileo's accounts of his early
experiments bored a lot of people, too. Who could get excited
over a man telling about rolling a lot of little metal balls
down an inclined plane and clocking the times of their de-
scent? Nobody, except a fellow scientist. Yet these dry-
as-dust laboratory experiments with the cards, the dice, and
the pictures will someday—someday not too far distant—turn
out to be even more momentous for the life of the human
race than were the equally matter-of-fact experiments of Galileo and Copernicus.

Just what have the parapsychologists done? They have
demonstrated experimentally the existence of a spiritual component in life and in the individual which is limited neither
by *distance* nor *time*. Past, present, and future have no meaning for it. Space has no meaning for it.

This is highly significant for our purpose here, because it

means that, for the first time in human history, science has demonstrated experimentally the existence of a part of the human personality which, since it is not limited by time and space, can conceivably survive that coming to a halt in time and space which we call death. And if science says there actually *is* such a component in life, then great added weight is given to the findings of the earlier psychical researchers who claimed that (through phantasms, mediums, cross-correspondences, and book tests) they had *contacted* such a surviving component on the other side of the grave. Previously, skeptics could deny the evidence from psychical research on the grounds that it had not been shown that there was anything in the human personality capable of surmounting the time-space barrier of death. But the skeptic can no longer say that. Perhaps the most momentous words yet uttered in the twentieth century were those spoken in Town Hall, New York, recently by Dr. Rhine: "According to minimum standards, the soul theory has been confirmed."

That there is a spiritual component in life and in the individual which *can* conceivably live on after the death of the body has now been proven conclusively in the laboratories of science itself. For the first time in history, immortality—the survival of consciousness after death—is at least a reasonable *speculative hypothesis* for science.

Professor R. H. Thouless of Cambridge University sums up the findings of parapsychology as follows:

> The reality of the phenomena must be regarded as proved as certainly as anything in scientific research can be proved. . . . Let us now give up the task of trying to prove again to the satisfaction of the skeptical that the "psi" effect really exists, and try instead to devote ourselves to the task of finding out all we can about it.*

*See J. B. Rhine, *The Reach of the Mind* [New York: William Sloane Associates, 1947], p. 172.

*. . . let the spiritual, unbidden and
unconscious, grow up through the common.*
—W. H. Channing

8

ARE YOU PSYCHICALLY SENSITIVE?

THIS BUSINESS OF MEDIUMSHIP IS ADMITTEDLY A MYSTE-
rious and baffling thing. A great many people secretly believe
that they have some unusual psychic sensitivity; numbers of
them have initiated a conversation with me by saying: "Now,
I've never said anything about this to anybody, but—" and have
gone on to confide some psychic experience of theirs which
would seem to indicate mediumistic ability. And most of us
have had brief and often commonplace experiences which
can be explained only on the basis of some psychic communication: you utter a remark at the same time that your companion utters the same remark; you decide to phone a friend
whom you have not called in weeks and just as you reach the
phone it rings—your friend is calling you; you think of an
aunt and wonder why she hasn't written to you for months,
so you sit down and write to her; as you are going out to
mail your letter the postman hands you a letter from your
aunt. Your dog is lying before the fireplace, apparently
asleep, and you think about calling to him to come over to
your chair. But before you can utter his name he raises his
head alertly and obeys your unspoken command. (Some students of animal psychology believe that dogs communicate
telepathically and can anticipate the commands of their mas-
ters by telepathic means!) Or you are suddenly smitten with a
vague uneasiness about the welfare of the baby, who is asleep

upstairs in a crib. You don't know why, but you just feel that you had better go up and look at the baby. So, feeling a little foolish, you do. Good thing, too—the baby has thrown off all the covers and is lying damply in a draft that blows in through the open window.

All this is by way of saying that many of us, perhaps most of us, are far more "psychic" than we realize. Professor William James used to say that we employ only about one-half of our actual powers and capacities in the business of living. We all have great resources upon which we never draw. The parapsychologists tell us that a psychic sensitivity is rudimentary in all of us, probably, but highly developed in only a few. Anthropologists point out that many primitives seem to be psychic: the mysterious "jungle telegraph" by means of which news flies through the vast wasteland at incredible speed is a *telepathic* phenomenon.

The questions may fairly be asked: am *I* a psychic? Can I develop this rudimentary power to the place where I can use it, perhaps even to the place where I can communicate with those on "the other side," just as Mrs. Piper, Mrs. Soule, and the others did?

Within certain limitations, the answer to both of these questions is a cautious yes. The rudimentary power can be developed, but it is not easy (though easier for some than others), and those who can develop the sensitivity to the point attained by Mrs. Piper will be few. But psychic sensitivity, like the other elements in man's spiritual nature, can be nurtured and developed. Any non-material discipline can be strengthened by constant practice, as the lives of saints and holy men throughout the ages remind us. The power of faith is a very real and living thing, and it can transform life.

What are the concrete steps that can be taken to bring out one's psychic sensitivity?

1. *You must sincerely believe in the reality of the spiritual world and the possibility of using the resources of the mind to contact it and to understand it.*

Here, as everywhere else in life, the Doubting Thomas is at a disadvantage. "Belief creates its own verification in fact," William James once said. "Only believe, and you shall see," go the words of an old hymn. "Faith can move mountains," says the Bible. The doubter will not be able to discover or use his untapped psychic resources until he gives up his doubt, for doubt is the acid that eats away at the foundation of the life of mind and spirit. *Commitment* is perhaps a better word than faith; the prerequisite for psychic experience is an emotional and intellectual commitment to spiritual truth, to the reality of the spiritual world.

How this principle works out in practice was clearly shown in experiments conducted by Dr. Gertrude Schmeidler in the psychology laboratory at the City College of New York. Dr. Schmeidler divided her students into two groups which she called "the sheep" and "the goats." The sheep were those who professed belief in psychic phenomena. The goats derided such belief. Both sheep and goats then took a long series of tests with the cards developed at Duke University for testing psychic ability. The sheep got positive (above chance) results, the goats got negative (below chance) scores.

2. *Test the degree of psychic sensitivity that you possess in the following ways:*

a. Using the cards developed for this purpose at Duke University (described at length in Chapter 7) test yourself for ability in telepathy, clairvoyance, and precognition.

To test *telepathy:* Have a friend shuffle the cards, then pick them up, one at a time, look at the symbol on each card, and place it face downward on the table. As he does this have him concentrate mentally on the symbol. You (who have not seen the face of the card) then call out the symbol which you think is on the face. Theoretically, you are getting your information about the symbol from the *mind* of your friend. Your friend then records your guess on a score sheet, recording the guesses in the order in which the cards are called and laid face downward on the table. After all twenty-five cards have been called, your guesses are checked against the actual order of the cards.

To test *clairvoyance,* neither you nor your friend looks at the face of the cards. He simply shuffles the deck and places it on the table. You then call out the order of the twenty-five cards in the deck as you believe it to be, and your friend records your "calls."

To test *precognition,* follow the same procedure as in the test for clairvoyance, except that in this case you do not "call" the order of the cards as you "see" them in the deck lying face down on the table, but as you think the order will be *after the deck is shuffled.* In other words, you look at the deck, close your eyes, and try to "look forward" in time and "see" the order of the deck as it will be after your friend has shuffled it.

In all of these tests, you can expect to call five of the cards correctly by chance alone. Five is the "chance expectancy" in all three. But, according to mathematical law, any score higher than five is above chance expectancy and statistically significant. In other words, if you score an average of five correct calls or less on any of these tests, it is an indication that you do not possess much psychic sensitivity. If you average between five and seven, it indicates some sensitivity beyond average. If you can consistently score above seven, it shows considerable psychic sensitivity on your part. A consistent score of ten or more shows exceptional ability which should be cultivated.

Now—the key word here is "consistent." You cannot judge your psychic sensitivity on the basis of one or even a dozen tests. From fifty to a hundred separate tests should be the minimum on which any kind of an estimate is made.

b. Using two simple Chinese checkerboards and the sets of colored marbles that go with them, test your precognitive powers in this way: Get a friend to agree that at a certain time (the next hour, the next day, the next week) he will arrange the marbles on one of the checkerboards into some sort of a design. You then arrange the marbles on the other board *as you think he will arrange them on the board he has at the agreed-upon time in the future.* When that time comes, compare your arrangement with his.

c. Using a pair of dice, test your psychokinetic ability (the use of psychic force to influence physical objects) by selecting a *target number*—say seven—and then seeing how many sevens you can throw. Twelve throws constitutes a run, and two sevens out of a run (twelve throws of the dice) is the chance expectancy. Any score beyond an average of two hits on the target per run is above-chance and therefore significant.

d. To test the power of your mind to influence physical objects in a non-statistical way, do this: Cut a square of light paper about 2″ by 2″. Fold it twice diagonally and then open it out until it looks like a small umbrella half-closed. Turn the bottom of a cardboard box upside down and punch a straight pin up through the middle of it. Rest the center of the paper umbrella lightly on the point of the pin, making sure that the umbrella does not touch anything but the pin and is evenly balanced. Place the whole arrangement on the table in front of you, making sure that there are no drafts which might move the paper, and that you are not breathing on it. Then, concentrate your mind on making the paper umbrella revolve. If you are doing it correctly and your "mind-force" is strong enough, you should eventually be able to make the umbrella turn both clockwise and counterclockwise, and at different rates of speed. You should also be able to make it stop at will. After you have done this, you can "fool-proof" the demonstration by placing the box, the pin, and the umbrella inside a deep glass bowl to eliminate any possibility of drafts or any accusation that you are really blowing on the umbrella. A variation of this experiment is to cut out a little cork boat, equip it with a paper sail, and use your mind-force to make it move in a dish of water.

There are lots of similar, simple experiments that you can conduct at home. For instance, stand two kitchen match sticks (the big ones) on end with a third one across the top, in the form of a small doorway. It may be that you will have to try different lengths and weights of matches before you will find a combination that will stand by itself. When you do get one that balances, try knocking it over by concentrating on it.

e. To test telepathy, or simple thought-transference without the use of cards or other physical devices, you might like to try the parlor game worked out in England some years ago by Professor Gilbert Murray. Professor Murray would go out of the room and, of course, out of earshot of the people in the room. Then someone in the room—preferably a very close friend or relative, one with whom he was *en rapport*—would think of a scene, or an incident, or anything at all, say it out loud for the benefit of the others in the room, and write it down. Then Professor Murray would be called back and would try to find out what had been thought of by telepathic means. To illustrate, here are some actual incidents, as recorded in *The Psychic Source-Book,* pp. 274-300:

(1) Mrs. Arnold Toynbee, a friend of the Murrays, thinks of the beginning of a story by Dostoevski where a poor old man's dog is dying in a restaurant.

Professor Murray comes back into the room and concentrates. Then he says: "I think it's a thing in a book. I should think a Russian book. A very miserable old man, and I think he's doing something with a dead dog. I think it's in a restaurant and people are mocking, and then they are sorry and want to be kind. I am not sure." (Mrs. Toynbee asks him about the nationality of the people) "No—I don't get their nationality. I have a feeling it is a sort of a Gorki thing. I have a feeling that it is something Russian."

(2) Mrs. Toynbee thinks of the Cornford children, Helena and Tony, grown up and walking beside the river at Cambridge.

Professor Murray returns to the room, concentrates, then says: "This is not a book. It's got a sort of Cambridge feel in it. It's the Cornfords somehow—no—it's a girl walking beside the river, but it isn't Frances (Mrs. Cornford). Oh! Is it baby Cornford grown up? Ought I to know what she is doing?" (Mrs. Toynbee: "Who is she with?" "No, I don't get who she is with—no—I should only be guessing." (Everyone in the room: "Go ahead and guess!") "No. I should only think of another baby grown up—Tony."

These illustrations will serve to show you how to play this telepathy game. Of course, Professor Murray didn't *always* hit the target as closely as he did in the two instances cited above, and neither will you. It is important that the agent (Mrs. Toynbee in the above cases) be someone fairly close to the person doing the "guessing," and it is important that everybody present keep quiet and that there are no distracting influences or noises.

f. The Bible observes that "The fathers have eaten sour grapes and the children's teeth are set on edge." This is not as fanciful as it sounds, and if you want to test the ability of the mind to experience a *sensation* that somebody else is having, do this: Take very small portions of such substances as vinegar, mustard, cloves, bitter aloes, sugar, etc. and *blindfold* two subjects. Then—being careful that there is enough distance between the two so that the substances can't be smelled—place a small amount of one of the substances on the tongue of one of the blindfolded persons. The other blindfolded person then tries to experience the taste or sensation telepathically and calls out what he thinks the substance is. To illustrate, here are some instances from such tests taken from *The Psychic Source-Book:*

TASTER	PERCIPIENT OR ONE WHO TRIES TO IDENTIFY THE TASTE	SUBSTANCE	ANSWER GIVEN
M	E	Vinegar	"A sharp and nasty taste"
M	E	Mustard	"Mustard"

M	E	Sugar	"I still taste the hot mustard"
EG and M	E	Worcestershire sauce	"Worcestershire sauce"
EG and M	E	Port wine	"Between eau de cologne and beer"
EG and M	E	Bitter aloes	"Horrible and bitter"
MG	R	Alum	"A taste of ink-of-vinegar. I feel it on my lips—it is as if I had been eating alum."

That will give you a general idea. The person with a high psychic sensitivity will be able to identify the different tastes better than half the time.

g. The final series of tests for psychic sensitivity that I am going to suggest is in the field of automatic writing. As previously indicated, the simplest device for testing your sensitivity in this area is the ouija board. You merely close your eyes and let the pointer under your hand move about the board of its own volition (apparently) and then see if what it spells out makes any sense. This was a parlor game that was very popular in the twenties, but many people grew tired of it because so much of what "came through" seemed to be gibberish. Of course it was gibberish; nine-tenths of what "comes through" even in the automatic speech and writing of trained mediums is gibberish. It takes patience and understanding to experiment with the automatisms, to sift the grain of gold from the sands of nonsense.

So—if you are patient, begin with the ouija board and see what you can make out of it. Then, if you like, go on to automatic writing *without* the ouija board.

It is not necessary to go into trance, or to be a medium in the usual sense in order to write automatically. Some dissociation is usually present, however. This means that you are, temporarily, not concerned with and perhaps not even aware of your surroundings. We speak of someone's being "lost in thought"; such a person is really *dissociated* and, unlike the medium in trance or the person who has been hypnotized, can be *associated*, or brought back to awareness of the surroundings with a word, or by hearing a dog bark, or the ringing of a doorbell.

So, the first step in automatic writing is the achievement of this slight dissociation. Some people slip into it quite naturally just by thinking about it; others can induce it by concentrating attention on some object: a pencil, a ring, a glass, etc., until they feel relaxed and slightly sleepy. Personally I have found that the necessary dissociation is present when I am half-awake, early in the morning, or when I come half-awake in the middle of the night.

When this dissociation is achieved and you are relaxed, you will find that your mental processes, which you might think would be slowed down, are really accelerated. Words, ideas, phrases, whole sentences will flow through your mind *if you are psychically sensitive,* and with some effort you can rouse yourself enough to write them down. They will literally tumble over themselves, and I have found that sometimes the mind gets exceedingly tired of this unaccustomed torrent and I come fully awake, nervous and irritable.

After writing down as best you can the words that rush through your mind, you will either come wide awake or go completely to sleep. No matter. If you have written down even a small part of what your stream of consciousness has produced, you will have an interesting record. You may need help to interpret it, however. And certainly most of it will be gibberish. But—if you are psychically sensitive—there may be discernible in the gibberish ideas, phrases, and sentences that make sense; that, according to psychical research, *may not have originated in your own mind at all,* but in the mind of someone not in the body who is taking advantage of your relaxed, receptive state and is trying to establish contact with you.

For instance: I am lying in bed at 5 A.M., brought half-awake by the sound of milk cans clattering on the pavement. My eyes are closed, but my mind is racing like a windmill. I am conscious of a vague *orange* light, but it is not yet dawn, and the *orange* feeling is in my consciousness. The words, phrases, and sentences tumble through my mind, and "something" says to me, "Write it down." By a great effort of will I reach the bedside table and get a paper and pencil. Heavily, reluctantly, almost painfully, I catch some of the racing words and, in the dark, write them down. I write like this, with that orange light all about me, for perhaps five minutes. Then the orange light fades; I come fully awake and am aware of the first gray streaks of dawn and the dim outlines of objects in the room. My hand aches from the effort of writing, but, when I am fully awake, I am hardly conscious of having done any writing at all. The whole episode is fleeing backward in memory—but I have the record, the heavy scribblings on the piece of paper. It goes something like this:

You are supposed but it didn't you know it isn't to go

Where there is no night there now nor morning here if it is in winter

But the school SCHOOL you never wanted and hurt on a nail

Like a ped remember and the ruler and the play money you didn't like it was Sylvia and the valentine but I sent you I sent you cried and all the games sister to New Street awful first time and the dog big dog you cut the lawn the little cards good fair bad all good blonde boy by the fire

You said you hurt me on a nail I sent you though remember

And the lunch always the condensed milk and cocoa the cereal lilac tree in the side yard but I sent you I sent you

A ped a ped a foot and George George street of a king and I sent you remember you hurt you on a nail I said it will feel better I sent you foot and George . . .

There was a lot more, but this was the only part of the record that made any sense at all to me. As a little boy I had attended a private school on George Street in Danbury, Connecticut, called "Miss Foote's." At this school we played "store" with play-money and play-groceries, and on Valentine's Day a girl named Sylvia brought me a big lacy valentine. I would frequently try to evade school by alleging to my mother that "I hurt me on a nail," but she always sent me off anyway, saying it would feel better after a while. At school we would get little cards at the end of the day with a single word on them: Good, Fair, or Bad. When I came home for lunch, I would usually have cocoa with condensed milk in it and cereal. My sister had gone to New Street public school and had hated it because she had to pass a yard with a big dog tethered in it.

Was this, in truth, my long-dead mother trying to identify herself? I would not categorically say so. But that is the way automatic writing works, and you can test your own ability at it, your own psychic sensitivity, in the same way I did.

What about the séance? Can a person who has reason to

believe that he or she is unusually psychic put on a séance with any hope of success?

Now, any meeting or session where an attempt is made to contact the non-material world is, strictly speaking, a séance. What I have described above is a séance, even though only one individual is involved. Of elaborate séances involving a large group of people, with mysterious rappings and material- izations, I am quite suspicious. There is too much room for fakery, conscious or unconscious. But the simple séances of mental mediumship—in which messages are sought and no attempt is made to mystify or materialize—are quite possible for one who has demonstrated unusual psychic sensitivity. A few close friends (the rapport is important), a closing of the eyes, a spiritual receptivity on the part of all, and the achievement of a light, self-induced trance state by the person most psychically sensitive—these are all that is necessary. From then on, whatever initiative there is will come from "the other side." We can only make ready the house; we can- not force the guest to come. Suffice it to say that the psychi- cally sensitive person who maintains the desired receptivity will have experiences that will confirm his or her belief in a spiritual world and its ongoing life.

3. If the scores compiled in these tests are consistently above average, and if you have had psychic experiences from time to time of strength and clarity, and if you sincerely wish to develop your psychic powers further, put yourself in the hands of a sound, reliable medium like Mrs. Eileen Garrett of the Parapsychological Foundation in New York, or a dis- tinguished teacher and researcher like Dr. Joseph B. Rhine of the Foundation for Research on the Nature of Man, Dur- ham, N.C. The technique of mediumship—the achievement of trance, etc.—can be learned like any other technique once the basic psychic sensitivity has been established. However, one must be careful to avoid "quacks" and "fakers"—and this is not always easy, for the field is full of them.

Philosophy will clip an angel's wings.
                                    —Keats

9

THE SCIENTIFIC
RETREAT FROM
MATERIALISM

WHEN THE POET JOHN KEATS MADE THE ABOVE OBSER-
vation, he meant *science* and not philosophy. Science, he was
saying, will clip the wings of theology and reduce religion to
naturalism. Keats was the child of his time, the nineteenth
century—the age of the Industrial Revolution and the worship of the machine. Little did the poet dream that by the
middle of the twentieth century science would be desperately
engaged in trying to stick the angel's wings back on again!

The same idea had been stated with much more emphasis
by another child of the nineteenth century, the father of Posi-
tivism, Auguste Comte. Comte held that there were three approaches to knowledge: the primitive or religious, based on
superstition, tradition, and dogma; the philosophical, based
on logical analysis; and the positivistic, or scientific, based on
direct observation. The latter would finally prevail. "When
science has done its complete work," he said, "it will conduct
God to the boundary of the universe and bow him out with
thanks for his provisional services."

Comte's cocksure statement remained an accurate description of the prevailing scientific temper until the Atomic Age,
when its inadequacies became terribly apparent to most scientists. But for the better part of its four-hundred-year-old history, modern science has been materialistic, mechanistic, and
anti-spiritual. It has refused to consider any phenomena that
could not be weighed, measured, analyzed, and reduced to pat
chemical, physical, or biological formulae. And by its refusal
it has, in effect, stamped all such phenomena as nonsense unworthy of the attention of intelligent men and women. Thus
the psychical phenomena of the ages—the folklore, the

hauntings, the poltergeists, the mediumistic experiences, the
automatisms—were never subjected to the classification,
correlation, and intensive study that the physical phenomena
received. They were ignored, or laughed out of court, or even
penalized by law. Certainly the climate—intellectual, legal,
and social—was not such as to encourage phenomena of this
nature, and yet they persisted, just as they had from the beginning of time. Not until the establishment of parapsychology as a university study in the second and third decades of
the twentieth century did modern science grant even a grudg-
ing hearing to the spokesmen for the non-material component
in life.

There were, of course, reasons for all this. Medieval science had no such bias against the non-material. The alchemists, astrologers, and philosophers of the Middle Ages—the
forerunners of modern science—had a healthy respect for the
spiritual world. Indeed, they sought its cooperation in their
various enterprises, and particularly in the two with which
they were the most preoccupied: the search for an "Elixir of
Life," a pure essence which could be applied to the body and
would make it perfect; and a "Philosopher's Stone," a universal solvent which would do for metals what purification did
for the soul. (They didn't find either one, but modern science
has come close to finding a "Philosopher's Stone" in the
atom!)

The alchemists and astrologers got along with only occasional brushes with the ecclesiastical authority because they
did not challenge the Church's officially proclaimed view of
the material world. This was the Aristotelian concept of a
flat earth with fixed stars. The conflict between the Church
and science began when post-medieval mathematicians like
Galileo challenged the Aristotelian, or Ptolemaic, conception
of the universe and insisted on the correctness of the Coper-
nican view. This challenge came in the year 1633. Shortly
thereafter the great independent universities were founded in
Florence, London, and Paris, and the scientists were free to
proceed without interference from the Church.

Galileo had been forced by the Inquisition to recant on his
knees for having the temerity to state that the earth revolved
around the sun, and not until 1835 were his works removed
from the Church's Index, or list of proscribed books. This
long struggle with the Church for the right to seek the truth
without regard for tradition or dogma had a lasting effect on
science. As a result of it, science left the Church and its dog-

mas strictly alone, establishing the "Great Divorce" between science and religion which was to continue until parapsychology, in our own day, built a bridge between the two.

Science, thus freed from the restraints of ecclesiastical authority, moved rapidly forward and soon had a long list of impressive accomplishments in its favor. Man's knowledge of the material world increased tremendously; all the great advances were technical and scientific. Religion, split by the Protestant Reformation, lapsed into static controversy and internecine warfare.

The Church was, at least in part, responsible for the fact that science ignored the realm of the spirit. It had at first denounced science in the name of the higher authority of the spiritual world, thus provoking an antispiritual temper in science, and then it had insisted that science limit its activities to its own domain—the material world—and leave the things of the spirit to priests and philosophers. Thus the Church insisted on a rendering unto Caesar of the things that were Caesar's and unto God the things that were God's, forgetting that what was Caesar's was also God's and also underestimating the wonderful things science would be able to do with what was rendered unto Caesar. Meanwhile, as the self-appointed custodian of what was God's, the Church promptly buried the spiritual treasure of mankind beneath a mass of dogmas, prohibitions, and creeds.

Science, limited both by inclination and by the still powerful authority of the Church to investigation of the material world, became increasingly inclined to regard mechanical principles as adequate explanations for just about everything in life, including human beings. An inevitable implication of this interpretation was the theory that what we call *mind*—indeed, anything non-material about man—was merely the by-product of the functioning of brain cells and nerve ganglia. All that we think of as mental, or spiritual, is nothing but a phase of the orderly working of the body chemistry. Love, hate, fear, joy, sorrow, exaltation, despair—art, literature, music, religion—pity, tenderness, sympathy—all these are incidental to and dependent on the proper functioning of the circulatory system and the ductless glands. In such a system, moral and religious ideas become not only inconsistent but intellectually disreputable. It is a closed system, with moral, ethical, and religious values left hanging outside, if indeed they are tolerated about the premises at all. Herbert Spencer argued that man can have no other destiny than that of the animal series from which he came; that the birth, growth, decline, and death of the physical body are paralleled in the mind. When the brain dies, thought ceases—it is a mere by-product of the functioning of the brain cells.

The most intelligent, humane, and logical expression of this closed mechanistic system was Charles Darwin's Theory of Evolution. It explained the role of natural causation—of how each manifestation of life could be traced back to one which preceded it. Evolution, as an explanation of how the human race got to where it is, was an intelligent and hopeful theory, for it pointed optimistically to a continuation of human progress toward ultimate perfection. Darwin was a great man and his principle of natural selection, although somewhat modified by later knowledge, stands today as just about the best explanation we have of the method by which we got to where we are. But Darwin himself was an agnostic, albeit a gentle one, and his theory became the principal creed of that increasingly formidable system of faith called "modern" science. For with its victories, of course, science slowly took on many of the less endearing characteristics of its old enemy the Church. To challenge its presuppositions and hypotheses became fully as dangerous as—in time, even more dangerous than—it had been back in Galileo's day to challenge the dogmas of the Church. Mesmer got as short shrift from the French Academy of Medicine as ever Luther did from the Diet at Worms, and when Harvey discovered the principle of the circulation of the blood he was denounced and laughed at by his medical colleagues. Freud was contemned by his fellow physicians in terms no less severe than Calvin used to castigate the Anabaptists.

Under the circumstances, the only way in which these two rival bodies of faith could coexist was by leaving each other strictly alone; by each proceeding without regard for the other. Yet both could not be right. Either there *was* a spiritual component in life or there was not; either there was a Plan and a Planner (God) or there was a pure mechanism fortuitously put in operation by accident. There could not be both. Science and religion were like two trains running on parallel sets of tracks in the same direction. One set of tracks led to the next station on mankind's strange itinerary through the universe and the other ended up against the side of a mountain somewhere. Unless somebody flagged down the train that was on the dead-end track or switched it over onto the track that led to the station, there would be an awesome crash someday. The trains would never collide, but one of them would ram itself into the mountain of reality and be destroyed. Meanwhile, science, the streamlined Super-Chief, thundered down the rails at 100 miles an hour, while religion, the Yaphank local, chugged mournfully from whistle-stop to whistle-stop.

There was no doubt but what, at this point, everybody that was anybody was aboard the express. The technical achievements of the closed mechanistic system of science were almost beyond imagination. Pain was ameliorated, disease conquered, the life-span extended. Everything was made cheaper and easier. The internal combustion engine and electricity foreshortened the distances of sea, sky, and earth. One man in the twentieth century, abetted by scientific gadgets, could do the work that had engaged thirty men in his grandfather's day. With a submachine gun he could kill as many of his fellows in five seconds as grandpa had been able to do in a full twenty-four hours with the öld breech-loader. With the new Bendix, mother could wash more clothes in two hours than her grandmother had been able to do in two weeks. Science had invented a steam hammer that could pulverize a locomotive or crack a nut-shell so tenderly that the kernel came out whole. Little wonder that the richest, smartest, most personable passengers all preferred the express to the local. Even many of the poor passengers in the latter yearned for the day when they could transfer to the shiny streamliner, swap their prayer-books for Martini cocktails, and go barreling toward eternity at 100 miles an hour. Some tried jumping from one train to the other in full flight, one or two successfully but most with lamentable results. A few even attempted to straddle the tracks and ride with one foot in each train. For a short ways, it was a surprisingly good trick.

The spectacle had its overtone of comedy, but it was essentially tragic. It was tragic because it divided not only the mind of man but all his most basic institutions. His law, his education, his moral and ethical standards of conduct, his social mores—all were still based on the pre-scientific concept of man as a responsible, autonomous personality possessed of an immortal soul. Thus, from the standpoint of science man was a mechanism subject to no law save natural principle; but in the eyes of the codified civil and criminal statutes, education and religion, he was a semi-divine being subject to laws, principles, standards, and dogmas all based on the assumption that he was something just the opposite of what

biology, chemistry, and physics said he was! Thus on the
same university campus one might find separate colleges of
medicine, law, science, education, and theology, two of them
(medicine and science) teaching that man was a pure mechanism whose law was in his own members, so to speak—his
brain cells, his nervous system, etc.— and three others (law,
education, and theology) teaching that he was a non-
mechanistic being possessed of mind and soul and subject to
a moral law which, for the faculties of medicine and science,
had no reality whatsoever! On one side of the campus man
was a mechanism and on the other side he was a free soul.
The professors of these various schools mingled with the
greatest of ease at the faculty teas, but many a poor, truth-
seeking student fell haplessly into the bottomless pit that bi-
sected the academic lawns. And when in his neurotic despair
he turned to a psychoanalyst for help, that worthy, long on
theory and short on practical experience, more often than not
advised him that a judicious fracture of the moral and civil
law via a more active sex-life was all that he needed.

The French philosopher Ernest Renan once predicted that
men in the twentieth century would spend a good part of
their time putting back together what men in the nineteenth
century had smashed. As far as science goes, this is certainly
true. The middle of the twentieth century finds science in full
retreat from the mechanistic outlook that characterized it in
the nineteenth and early twentieth centuries. God, whom
Comte ushered politely to the door of the universe, is now
back in the living room and very much at home. Indeed, the
prediction of Steinmetz that the greatest scientific discoveries
of the twentieth century would be in the realm of the spirit is
now in a fair way to being proved true.

As previously indicated, one reason for the sharp decline
in the popularity of materialism was the rise of psychology.
Psychology was itself a prisoner of the mechanists (with
some notable exceptions like McDougall) but the studies of
Freud, Jung, and others *did* shake the smugness of those who
insisted that the universe and everything in it, including the
human mind, were pure mechanisms. The streamliner rushed
on, but with diminished speed and the beginning of controversy in the club car.

Another reason for the decline of the mechanist hypothesis
was the creation of the atom bomb and the experiments in
nuclear fission that led up to it. A French philosopher once
expressed gratitude to God for "the good news of damna-

tion"; for many scientists the atom bomb was "the good news of damnation." The official War Department report on the first atomic explosion at Alamogordo Air Base in New Mexico states that after the blast the assembled scientists shook hands and that "the feeling was one of profound awe." It had been a long time since science had experienced awe. But after Alamogordo, Hiroshima, and Nagasaki—after the blasts which, in the words of *Time* magazine, "created a bottomless wound in the conscience of the race," many intelligent scientists began to see the tragic absurdity of the divorce between science and religion. The light of the atomic explosion showed clearly that it was the Diesel-powered streamliner of science that was rushing down the dead-end track. Professor Harold Urey, who had helped develop the bomb, wrote a pamphlet called *I Am a Frightened Man*. And Dr. Robert Oppenheimer, when asked by a congressional committee whether or not there was any protection against the bomb, replied: "Yes." "What is it?" cried the legislators. "Peace," said Oppenheimer quietly.

A chorus of scientific *mea culpa* filled the air. If the only defense against annihilation was in the realm of the spirit, if what Santayana termed "the soul's invincible surmise," was the only defense left to the human race—then, surely, that realm of the spirit must be real and that "invincible surmise" must be true. If only the spiritual component in man, his "soul," could now defend him against atomic extinction, then in the final analysis (and this was about as final as it was possible to get) that spiritual component was not only real, it was the *most real* thing in the whole cosmos!

A writer, arguing recently against immortality, cites as evidence the fact that Professor James Leuba took a poll of a thousand scientists sometime in 1914 and discovered that only 50.6 per cent of them believed in any kind of a life after death.*

It seems to me that this has quite an opposite significance to that attributed to it in the treatise. For more than half of one thousand scientists, indoctrinated with the stark mechanism of late nineteenth and early twentieth century science, to express a belief—even a qualified belief—in the existence and immortality of the soul is a rather striking testimony to the power of faith. It is as though a poll of the So-

---

*Corliss Lamont, *The Illusion of Immortality* [New York: The Philosophical Library, 1950].

viet Politburo should disclose the fact that more than half the comrades believed in the principles of Trotsky. And if such a poll were to be made of scientists today, after the rise of parapsychology and the wave of atomic disillusionment which has swept science, it is almost certain that the percentage of scientific believers would be much higher.

Among the scientists who are proclaiming their faith in God and His purpose in life today is Dr. Arthur H. Compton, Nobel prize-winner in physics and director of the Metallurgical Atomic Project during World War II. Dr. Compton states unequivocally that "there can be no question of God's existence."*

The world, he holds, has not made itself. Forces operating in nature over which we have no control were responsible for the gradual development of life until that development culminated in man. What are these forces over which we have no control? Dr. Compton calls them "God." Science, he says, is concerned with understanding the way in which this higher force (God) operates. It is concerned with what happens in life, with the actions that occur, and with the laws that govern those actions. But *action* implies an *actor*. That actor behind the observable action is God. Darwin's natural causation, says Dr. Compton, shows us how life evolved to its present state but not *who* or *what* started it going and *why*. He quotes Isaac Newton, as paraphrased by the poet Alfred Noyes:

> 'Tis not the lack of links within the chain
> From cause to cause, but that the chain exists;
> That's the unfathomable mystery,
> The one unquestioned miracle that we *know,*
> Implying every attribute of God.†

To Dr. Compton, the study of natural science is the primary source of the raw material for building our idea of God.

Another modern scientist of the highest reputation who unhesitatingly asserts his belief in God and his faith in the primacy of the spirit is Dr. A. Cressy Morrison, former president of the New York Academy of Sciences. Science, says

*From the Garvin Lecture for 1940 entitled "The Idea of God As Affected by Modern Knowledge" [Lancaster, Penn.].

†From Alfred Noyes, *Watchers of the Sky* [New York: J. B. Lippincott Co., 1922].

Dr. Morrison, has made stupendous discoveries in the ninety years since Darwin wrote his *Origin of the Species*. These discoveries have brought it closer to an awareness of God. Dr. Morrison gives seven reasons for his own personal faith.*

1. *It is possible to demonstrate mathematically that the universe could not have just happened, but was designed purposively.*

To illustrate: Put ten pennies or pieces of cardboard or whatnot, marked from one to ten, in your pocket. Shuffle them up without looking at them. Now see if you can take them out in sequence—number one first, number two second, number three third, and so forth. Mathematically, your chance of drawing number one first would be one in ten; of drawing numbers one and two in succession one in ninety; of drawing numbers one, two, and three in succession, one in 720; etc. You would have just one chance in 3,628,800 of drawing all ten numbers in their right order!

Now—there are so many exacting conditions and delicately balanced circumstances necessary for life to exist at all on earth, that the odds against their existing in proper relationship by chance alone are much greater than your chance of pulling numbers one through ten out of your pocket in the right order. For instance—the earth rotates on its axis at 1,000 miles per hour. If it rotated at only 100 miles per hour, our days and nights would be ten times as long as they are now, and the earth would alternately burn and freeze. Under such circumstances, vegetation could not live. Again—the sun has a surface temperature of 12,000 degrees Fahrenheit and our earth is at the exact distance from it that it needs to be to get just enough heat and not too much. The earth is tilted at an angle of 23 degrees and this enables us to have four seasons; if it were not tilted at this angle, vapors from the ocean would move north and south piling up continents of ice. If the moon were not at the exact distance it is from the earth, the ocean tides would inundate the land mass completely twice a day. If the ocean were just a few feet deeper than it is, the carbon dioxide and oxygen in the earth's atmosphere would be completely absorbed and no vegetable life could exist on earth. If the earth's atmosphere were just a little thinner, many of the meteors which are now burned out in space would bombard us, setting great fires everywhere.

*See A. Cressy Morrison, *Man Does Not Stand Alone* [New York: Fleming H. Revell Co., 1944].

Did this delicate balance just happen? Not a chance in ten million, says Dr. Morrison.

2. *The resourcefulness of life is a sign of a directing Intelligence.*

Nobody knows what life is. You can't weigh or measure it, and yet it conquers all the elements and reforms them to suit itself. The life of a frail plant cannot be seen, but it can crack a rock. Life is a sculptor which shapes all living things; a musician that teaches birds, insects, and men to sing; a chemist which gives taste to fruit and spices, perfume to flowers, and transforms water and carbonic acid into sugar and wood. A transparent, mistlike drop of protoplasm, drawing energy from the sun, holds the seed of all life and is the mother of everything that lives, both plant and animal. Where did it come from? *Nature* did not create it—fire-blackened rock and a saltless ocean, the earth before life appeared on it, lacked the necessary materials for producing it. Who, then, put it there? Who else but God?

3. *The wisdom of nature testifies to a Creator Who is good.*

Whence came that mysterious animal radar that we call "instinct"? The young salmon stays at sea for years, and then comes back to the river, to the very tributary, to the very shallow where he was born. Pick him up and put him down in another tributary and he will know at once that he is in alien waters and will battle his way back to his own tributary and then up against its current until he is where he belongs. Eels, at maturity, go unerringly to the depths of the ocean off Bermuda from all the rivers and ponds everywhere. They come out of little, obscure ponds and lakes far inland, swim down brooks, rivers, and bays to the ocean, cross the ocean, and arrive off Bermuda. Here they breed and die. And the newborn baby eels, who apparently can know nothing except that they are in the depths of the ocean somewhere, and who cannot communicate with each other, immediately start back for the exact pond or river from which their parents came. No American eel has ever been caught in European waters, and no European eel has ever been caught in American waters. Moreover, nature has delayed the maturity of the European eel by a full year to make up for its longer journey. Eels never make mistakes. Where did they get that unerring impulse?

Or, take the wasp. The wasp conquers a grasshopper and stings the grasshopper in exactly the right spot, so that the grasshopper becomes unconscious but does not die. Then the wasp lays her eggs at just the right distance from the unconscious grasshopper so that her young can nibble the preserved meat without quite killing the grasshopper! Putrid meat would be fatal to them. The mother, however, knows that everything is all right. She flies off and dies. It all had to be done right the very first time, or there would be no wasps in the world at all. Adaptation, says Dr. Morrison, cannot explain such techniques. The only explanation is that they were *bestowed* by a Divine Intelligence.

4. *Instinct is wonderful, but man has in addition to instinct the power of reason.*

Man is the only member of the animal kingdom to possess this power. Man alone can see himself in relation to the rest of the universe; man alone can use thought to project himself forward or backward in time. Nothing else in the universe can even count up to ten, let alone know what "ten" means. Instinct is like a single, beautiful flute-note, whereas reason provides man with all the notes and combination of notes needed for a performance of Bach's *B-Minor Mass*. The only explanation for this *reason* is that it is a spark of the superior Reason that created it.

5. *Since Darwin we have learned a great deal about the wonders of the genes.*

There are some two billion people in the world. Yet the genes and chromosomes from which they all come and which contain every biological characteristic of every one of them could be put in a thimble. How do these tiny genes enclose within themselves all the hereditary features of multitudes of ancestors and preserve the psychology of each in such a microscopic space? How these little genes can provide for all life on earth is a question that can have but one answer—it was *planned* that way. And a plan must have a Planner.

6. *The economy of nature is explicable only on the basis of infinite wisdom.*

In Australia, a species of cactus was planted as a protective fence. However, this cactus had no natural enemies in Australia, so it flourished to such an extent that it threatened to engulf farms and even whole towns. An area approximately the size of England was taken over by the cactus. Entomologists searched everywhere for a natural enemy to oppose the growth of the cactus, and finally discovered an insect that lived exclusively on cactus. This insect also had no natural enemies in Australia and so was able to breed freely there.

The insect slowly pushed back the cactus and today insect and cactus are in perfect balance in Australia. We see such marvelous checks and balances throughout nature. Without them, fast-breeding insects would long since have taken over the earth. For instance—insects have no lungs such as man has; they breathe through tubes. But the tubes do not grow larger as the insect grows, thus preventing the development of big insects. Without this natural restriction on the size of the insect's breathing apparatus, man would long since have lost his battle with the tiny creatures.

7. *Man's mind is proof of God.*

Man is the only thing in the universe that *can* conceive the idea of God. Can mind develop out of the mindless? Can the created be greater than the Creator? No. The fact that man can use his mind to conceive the idea of God is the very best proof that God is. "God is everywhere and in everything," concludes Dr. Morrison, "but nowhere so close as in our hearts."

Another eloquent scientific affirmation of God comes to us from the late Dr. Pierre Lecomte du Noüy, physicist and Nobel prize-winner, who testifies to the reality of the spiritual world in his great book, *Human Destiny.**

Evolution, he says, always proceeds from the most highly developed organ at any given stage. This means that from here on, life will evolve toward a higher stage from the human brain, the mind, the consciousness, for the accomplishment of *consciousness* is the newest and greatest achievement of the evolutionary process. In other words, at the apex of evolution man has achieved a spiritual component, or soul, and from this point on, while his body may continue adapting itself to the conditions of life, it will be along the lines of this spiritual component that his evolutionary progress will proceed. The great discoveries of tomorrow will not be in the realm of biochemistry or nuclear physics, but in the field of the so-called psychic, the extrasensory. This theory Dr. du Noüy calls tele-finality (ultimate purpose). He talks about "the untiring effort to draw nearer to God," and concludes that "the destiny of man is not limited to his existence on earth and he must never forget that fact." Life, he says, did not just happen; it was *willed.* It is as intentional a creation as the skyscraper.

Compton, Morrison, and du Noüy are only a few of the oustanding modern scientists who have abandoned material-

*New York: Longmans, Green & Co., 1947.

ism and are calling for a return to God and a new faith in the reality of spirit. Erwin Schroedinger, Alexis Carrel, Robert Millikan, L. P. Jacks, Arthur Eddington, James Jeans, and many others are calling for a renewed and revivified faith in God and the spiritual world. They agree with Francis Bacon, who wrote:

> I had rather believe all the fables in the Legend, and the Talmud, and the Alcoran, than that this universal frame is without a mind; and, therefore, God never wrought miracles to convince atheism, because his ordinary works convince it. It is true that a little philosophy inclineth Man's mind to atheism, but depth in philosophy bringeth men's minds about to religion; for while the mind of Man looketh upon second causes scattered, it may sometimes rest in them, and go no farther; but when it beholdeth the chain of them confederate, and linked together, it must needs fly to Providence and Deity.*

Edward Young wrote that "an undevout astronomer is mad," and the great Johannes Kepler himself, as he watched the motion of the stars through his telescope, declared that he "was thinking the thoughts of God after him."

All these arguments which have brought distinguished men of science to God, are arguments *from design*. Via design is the only way for a good scientist to come to God, and the argument from design is a very good argument. But for this writer, at least, nature—wonderfully formed and marvelously interdependent as it is—is too impersonal, too objective, too non-moral to provide a final and conclusive argument for the existence of God and the immortality of the human soul. The entire drive of the whole awe-inspiring machine—or at any rate that part of it which is observable here on earth—seems to be directed largely to one simple end—pollination. Life's drive to perpetuate itself cuts squarely across all the moral, ethical, and other values customarily associated with religion. And yet life's drive to perpetuate itself must be the very hub of the divine design, if design there be!

Also, the argument from design leaves unsolved the great, central problem of man's existence on this planet—the problem, the paradox, of Good and Evil.

A correspondent, arguing against theism, writes: "If a God really does exist, how do you account for evil? Why did God

---

*Francis Bacon, *Essays* [London: A. Steele Co., 1867], p. 169.

create Hitler, cockroaches, Gerald L. K. Smith, and the bu-
bonic plague? And why doesn't He do something about the
New York subway system?"

The question is facetious, but the problem it raises is cru-
cial. It is a paradox that has absorbed the theologians from
St. Paul on down to Sören Kierkegaard and the French Exis-
tentialists. Life is good and bad, light and dark, lustful and
loving, peaceful and murderous. Why? A Bible moralist
piously proclaims that he "has never seen the righteous hungry or his seed begging bread." He should have been living in
the city of Chicago during the depression years, or on a ten-
ant farm in Arkansas during the late thirties. As a minister
and social worker, this writer has seen many of the righteous
hungry—hungry and forced to suffer the added indignity of
being lectured by the unrighteous, who were usually well-fed.
Human misery is too vast to be explained away on the basis
of piousness or lack of it, righteousness or lack of it, or even
"right mental attitude" or the lack of it. To say that God,
having created all things, gave man free will and that man
thereupon brought into being and chose evil, is too pat. The
"first cause" of the evil would still be the God who brought
into being a creature capable of creating and choosing evil as
over against good. And the doctrine of Original Sin—"In
Adam's fall we sinned all"—is obviously not going to be accepted by intelligent men and women who know very well
that Adam was a tiny droplet of protoplasm.

No, the argument for God from design is a great and basic
argument, but it cannot cope adequately with the problem of
Good and Evil. At that point, science must yield to those
lesser authorities, philosophy and religion. But—is there not a
science, or a system employing the scientific method, that
bridges the gap between the scientific argument from design
and the philosophical and religious explanation of the problem of Good and Evil?

It seems to me that parapsychology is that science. It provides us with *evidence* of the spiritual world, that world of
warmth and beauty and creativity and love that lies just beyond the fingertips; that world which, in the words of the
poet Dante, is "so strong to fight against all that is false and
low and mean in life"; that world of which the great souls of
the ages give such eloquent testimony—Prince Gautama,
Lao-tse, King David, Jesus, St. Francis, Gandhi. And it is
that revealed world of thought and feeling in which our true
citizenship lies, and in which our most meaningful and mem-

orable experiences of life are founded. The question of the attributes of God, the answer to the problem of Good and Evil, we may well leave to the philosophers and theologians. When we know that we are the inhabitors of "a house not made with hands eternal in the heavens," we are able to await the answers with calm confidence. It is not our purpose here to go into them; suffice it to say that there *are* answers. Having established (as I think we have) that there is a design and a Designer, and having established that there is a spiritual component, or *soul,* in man which is independent of space and time, and having found in parapsychology a bridge between the science that affirms the design and the philosophy and theology that define the Designer, let us rest.

But our subject here is immortality. We have shown that science, or at any rate many scientists, has come to believe in God through an awareness of *design* in the universe. But does this belief in God necessarily postulate a belief in immortality?

Yes. Human consciousness is too great an accomplishment to be snuffed out as though it had never been after less than one brief century of existence. As du Noüy has shown, the whole end of the evolutionary process to date, proceeding slowly through eons, has been the achievement of consciousness. And consciousness (spiritual component, soul, mind) is a singular of which there is no plural, as Dr. Erwin Schroedinger, of the Dublin Institute of Advanced Studies, points out in his book *What Is Life?**

> A God, who, having bestowed the gift of consciousness on His creation, should then capriciously limit it or make it subject to accident or happenstance, would certainly not be the God of the intricate and majestic design of nature. Even less would He be the God whose very name is a contraction of the word Good.

Also, unless immortality is a fact, then God is in much the same position as the operator of a dog race, who entices the animals to run by keeping an electrically operated mechanical rabbit a few feet in front of them. In that case, the hope of eternity would be the deceptive gadget that keeps the human race plunging down its allotted three score years and ten. We may sometimes think (as many profess) that men would lead as good, honest, ethical lives without the hope of immortality

---

*Subtitle: *The Physical Aspect of the Living Cell* [New York: The Macmillan Co., 1945].

as they do with it, but we would be guilty of overestimating man as a biological animal. Deprive him of his soul and his expectation, however faint, of its survival of bodily death, and you will have cut the nerve that gives meaning to life. Life would go on, but it would be an empty thing if we believed that there were no values that were not transitory and no morality that was not relative. The divine sanction that gives life significance would disappear with positive assurance that life ends in the grave or the crematorium.

I have pointed out earlier that most men do not believe in immortality merely on the basis of philosophical and religious affirmation of it, that they do not live *actively* as though it were a fact. This is true, but they do not live in *disbelief* of it either. If they do not believe it any longer because philosophers and theologians tell them it is so, neither have they given it up altogether as a vestigial remnant of an outmoded Age of Faith. What they (we) are doing is living in a sort of a state of suspended judgment about it, afraid to disbelieve and yet lacking the scientific knowledge (the only kind we have any faith in) to affirm. Thus we live at half-speed, failing to realize our spiritual potentialities, but keeping just ahead of bleak Nihilism.

Finally, also as indicated before, it is impossible to postulate a *moral* God without at the same time postulating another life beyond this one, a life in which there is some opportunity to correct the manifold injustices of this existence. That Truth should forever (or at least a good bit of the time) be on the scaffold while Error sits proudly on the throne, is a state of affairs that is utterly incompatible with the moral nature of good. We do not mind the mills of the gods grinding slowly, if only they ultimately *do* grind exceedingly fine, but if they don't, then we are tempted to follow the misbegotten advice of the friends of Job and "curse God and die."

No, the immortality of the spiritual component, the individual human soul, is the inevitable corollary of a belief in God, no matter by what route we come to that belief. When Dr. J. B. Rhine made his memorable statement in Town Hall that "The soul theory has been confirmed," he followed it with another statement. "In a similar speculative way, we can now at least rationally conceive of the existence of a universal spirit equivalent to the modern conception of God."*

*"The Relation Between Psychology and Religion," a talk broadcast from Town Hall, New York, June 11, 1946 on the World Faith Round Table series.

To this the eminent scientists cited in this chapter would add a reverent Amen. And many of them would answer the age-old question "If a man die, shall he live again?" as the French philosopher Jacques Maritain does:

> In point of fact, will the aspiration of the human Person, of the entire man toward immortality remain forever unsatisfied? No, this aspiration will not remain unsatisfied, the soul and body will be reunited, this same Person, this identical human Person whom we knew and loved during our evanescent days, is actually immortal; this undivided human totality that we designate by a man's name will perish for a while, yes, and will know putrefaction; yet in reality and when all is said and done he will triumph over death and endure without end.*

*"The Immortality of Man," the Garvin Lecture for 1941, from the book *Man's Destiny in Eternity* [Boston: Beacon Press, 1949].

"In all this," replied Don Quixote, *"I must inform thee, friend Sancho, that there is no remembrance which time will not deface, nor no pain to which death will not put a period."*

"Thank you for nothing," quoth Sancho

—Cervantes

10

THE SOUL AND
THE SAVAGE

THANKS FOR NOTHING! THAT IS THE UNIVERSAL REACTION of what Mark Twain used to call "the damned human race" to assurances that all its cares and woes will be assuaged in the long sleep of the grave. To all poetic talk of "sweet death," to all philosophical rhetoric about the immortality of deeds and the river that one day reaches the sea, poor old bedeviled humanity replies, "Thanks for nothing."

We are grateful to the poets, philosophers, and theologians for dressing up the ferryman of the Styx so attractively, but we still are loath to make the trip. Death may end our woes, but we'd rather have our woes, thank you. At least, long association has made them familiar to us. And as for that river that someday meets the sea—well, if we do have to die, we don't want to get our little human personalities merged and lost in some great divine ocean. When we *are* finally clubbed and keelhauled out of this vale of tears, we want to be the same persons that we have been here in this life. In other words, aside from certain mystics and saints among us, we all yearn for personal and individual immortality. Group immortality, the immortality of memory and good deeds done, may be all very well for sociologists; and the merging of all personality in a union with the Divine Source may appeal to Christian mystics and Hindu holy men. But immortality of that sort will not satisfy most of us. We want to retain the essential *I* beyond the grave, with all its rich and special associations and emotions. Anything less is not immortality as far as the average human being is concerned. When that "roll is called up yonder," we would rather not be present, but if we have to be we'd like to be there *in person* to answer to the old, familiar name that has distinguished us from every other human being during our lifetime. Moreover, we'd like to hear other old, familiar names and look upon the faces of those whom we "have loved long since, and lost awhile"—the baby brother who died in infancy, the sweetheart killed in the war, Aunt Jennie, Grandma and Grandpa, Mother and Father.

To the philosopher, sage, and saint this may not be a very dignified conception of immortality. But it is what most human beings want. What are the chances of getting it? We are taking a long, square look at that question in this book, but it may help us to understand what we are looking at if we turn our attention briefly to our primitive ancestors and see what they thought about it.

For, of course, they did think about it. It is the oldest and greatest of all human themes from the beginning of time to the present; the inspiration of the noblest music, the most beautiful art, the most moving literature; the subject of the most profound speculation; the basis alike of mankind's deepest despair and fondest hope. The archeologists find fragments of the Great Theme scratched on the walls of the most ancient tombs, and the anthropologists find it running like a constant leitmotiv through the cultures of the most primitive tribes in the most remote places of earth. Men everywhere, and in all times, have asked the question that Job asked: "If a man die, shall he live again?"

Indeed, the anthropologists tell us that our cave-dwelling forbears were concerned about immortality before they were concerned about God! Every primitive tribe repeats in its own history the whole history of the race, and there are tribes, like the Gnanji of Central Australia, which do not have any gods but do have a doctrine of the immortality of the soul. The Gnanji are so backward that they have never developed any theology, but they believe profoundly in a kind of reincarnation. A child, they hold, is merely a dead person who has come to life; the souls of the dead wait around to be reborn and they do this by getting into the bodies of women and then being born normally. Thus the young women of the tribe are urged to foil the disembodied souls by pretending to be old and unable to give them (the souls) normal birth. The souls gather at certain places, and it is wise for the young women to either slip past these places without being noticed or to dress themselves up to look older than they actually are.

There is some evidence, therefore, that our concern with immortality is even older than our concern about God. This is

not too strange when we remember that it is the phenomenon
of death that stirs us more than anything else to ponder the
true nature of the universe and our place in it. Primitive man
could not help but observe that everybody died—the smart,
the dumb, the simpleton, the sage, the rich, the poor. Every
path in life led to the same place. Death came to every man,
and every man, no matter how proud or strong or rich, came
to death. To be born was to begin to die. The two experiences
were a part of the same process. Man had to make his peace
with the knowledge that he would surely die. In other words,
he had to become a philosopher. Socrates expressed the philosophy which had been forced on all mankind by the alterna-
tion and interplay of birth and death. "The Thirty Tyrants
have condemned you to death!" cried his friends. "And nature
them," replied the Sage of Athens calmly. Primitive man
came to see that nature had condemned him to death, and it is
not strange that this realization preceded his awareness of a
Power in the universe outside of himself and impelled him to
ponder on the nature of that Power.

The first answer that our primitive ancestors gave to the
question, "If a man die, shall he live again?" seems to have
been: he doesn't die, he gets killed. The very earliest savages,
the anthropologists tell us, believed in natural immortality—
that is, that unless something untoward happened to a man, he
would go on living forever. The Abipones (horse Indians of
Paraguay) believed that they would live forever if it were not
for Spaniards and sorcerers. They didn't die, they got killed.
Most savage tribes have held a similar belief at an early stage
in their development—that the enemy can kill by violence and
the sorcerer or witch by incantation, but that if these foes can
be outwitted, life will go on forever. As time goes on and the
savage sees that everybody does die, and as the instances that
cannot by any stretch of the imagination be attributed to enemies or sorcerers pile up, he reluctantly gives up his early belief in natural immortality and turns to finding some explanation of just how death got into the world.

Oddly enough, the science of biology today gives a small
amount of support to our poor old benighted ancestor and his
belief in natural immortality. Some biologists point out that
the most basic forms of plant and animal life, the highly organized, one-celled Infusoria, do keep on living and dividing
unless something steps in to stop the process. These biologists

hold that it was only the development of sexuality as the method of procreation that brought death to nature.*

Even today we find strong traces of this ancient belief in natural immortality in the teachings of modern religious groups, like the Christian Scientists, and in the more esoteric cults of the East. The manufacturers of certain vitamins also play around with the idea in their advertising copy, assuring us that we don't die but commit suicide with the knife and fork, an eventuality that can be inhibited, if not altogether prevented, by using their product.

This belief in natural immortality on the part of our primitive ancestors and their modern counterparts, the isolated savage tribes of Africa and the Pacific Islands, gave rise to some very interesting stories of how death did finally get into the world. The biologists who say that death came to the natural world with the principle of sexuality, and was an innovation introduced for the benefit of the race, are a pretty prosaic lot compared with the tribal medicine men. The latter really came up with some ingenious and poetic explanations.

A typical savage explanation of how death came to the world is found in the "Story of the Two Messengers," and is believed by the Bantu tribes of Africa. According to this story, the Unkulunkula (Old, Old One, or God) could not quite make up his mind whether he wanted people to die or not. He decided to send two messengers, one bearing a message reading, "Let the people live forever," and the other a message reading, "Let the people die," to the tribes on earth. The message which reached the people first should be the law.

Being somewhat sympathetic to the people, the Old, Old One entrusted the "Let the people live forever" message to a very fast creature, the chameleon. The "Let the people die" message was given to a much slower creature, the humble lizard. The chameleon jumped off to a huge lead, but grew overconfident and stopped off to eat some flies and have a little nap in the sun. As he slumbered peacefully in a tree, the lizard lumbered past with the message of death and reached the people well ahead of the chameleon. From then on, the people died. Even today, Bantu children, when they catch a chameleon, will torture it with sticks and upbraid it, shouting: "Why did you stop to sleep? Now we must all die!"

This story, in one form or another, is found in a great many

*See August Weismann, *Essays Upon Heredity and Kindred Biological Problems* [Oxford: Clarendon Press, 1889].

places, and apparently even Mr. Aesop was not unfamiliar
with it. The tale of the famous race between the tortoise and
the hare is a lineal descendant of the ancient story of the two
messengers.

Other tribes developed other stories. The natives of the
Banks Islands in the New Hebrides believe that originally people cast their skins like snakes and crabs, and thus kept on re-
newing life. When a man grew old, he simply cast off his old
wrinkled skin and stepped forth in the full bloom of youth.
However, this happy process was interrupted when an old
woman cast off her skin and threw it into the river, only to
find that her baby granddaughter did not recognize her when
she returned with her new, youthful skin. The baby cried and
the old woman, to pacify her, searched along the riverbank
for her old skin, found it, and put it back on. This pleased the
child but the gods took a dim view of the action and decreed
that from then on there should be no more skin-casting and
that people would just have to die.

In order to believe in immortality (once the concept of natural immortality had faded) our ancestors had to believe that
man had some kind of a *soul*, some part of his personality
which was able to survive the dissolution of the body in death.
Obviously the body "died" completely; there was no part of it
that endured forever, although the bones and skull lasted a
long time. Therefore, if anything survived the death experience, it must be something that couldn't be seen. Out of this
kind of reasoning grew the belief that the soul was a *spirit*,
and that every man had not only his body, which could be
seen, but his spirit, which could not be seen. Man was thus, in
this primitive view, both body and spirit. The body died, but
the spirit lived on. While the body lived the spirit dominated
it, driving it this way and that, and when the body died the
spirit left the body and went somewhere else—to Heaven, to
the Happy Hunting Ground, or into the bodies of living men
or animals. Almost all of this primitive dualism has survived
up to the present in some form.

The primitives thought of this soul in many ways. Some
thought of it as the little animal inside the big animal, and the
little man inside the big man, doing the directing and guiding.
Others thought of it as dwelling in various parts of the
body—in the heart, in certain glands, in the kidneys, in the
hair. The Old Testament story of Samson and Delilah is a
good illustration of the ancient belief that the hair is somehow
connected with the vital element. Some tribes associated the

spirit or soul with the shadow, and believed that if the shadow was tramped on, the body was injured. In southern latitudes, the noon-hour is the so-called "ghost-hour," because then the shadow is small and the vital energies are supposed to be at their lowest ebb. Still other tribes think of the soul as existing outside of the body, in a tree, plant, animal, or bird. "Totemism" is the name that anthropologists give to this belief in an external soul.

We are all familiar with the fact that many savage tribes are accustomed to burying weapons, food, etc. with the dead warrior so that he may have these necessities in the Happy Hunting Ground, or wherever he is. In the past, some tribes have carried this idea so far as to kill and bury women with the warriors to be their wives in the next world—a bit hard on the women, but quite logical. The ancient Druids even lent money to people which was to be repaid after death by their resurrected bodies! The concept here is of a next world, an eternity, which is very similar to this world, the world of Time. The soul, in this conception, is simply another version of the body, carrying on a life beyond the grave which is almost an exact replica of the life that was lived here. We find something rather like this in modern Mohammedanism, which also has a very materialistic idea of heaven.

Common to many of these primitive conceptions of the soul and its after-life state is a belief in some form of reincarnation or transmigration. We have already seen how the Gnanji tribe of Central Australia believed that the souls of the dead waited to get into the bodies of young females and achieve rebirth. Other tribes have held that the souls of the dead are reincarnated in animals, birds, and people. This belief in transmigration and reincarnation is held today by millions in our own world—by Hindus and other Far Eastern religious groups, as well as by Theosophists and Vedantists in the West. It will probably come as a surprise to the average Christian to be told that most of the world's people who believe in life after death hold to a faith in some kind of reincarnation, but that happens to be the case.

Yes, the oldest question that mankind knows anything about—older even than questions about God—is this: if a man die, shall he live again? It is a question so ancient and so universal that we may almost risk the ire of the psychologists and say that it is intuitive and instinctual; that a hunger for immortality is built into man just as are the hungers to eat and to procreate.

The first thing to note, then, in seeking an answer to this pervasive question is the fact that our primitive ancestors, from the very beginning of human history, believed that man lived in some form after death. Anthropology and archeology join to assure us that men everywhere, at all times since the beginning of time, have believed that they were possessed of immortal souls which, in one way or another, survived the universal experience of the body's death.

To philosophize is to learn to die.
                    —*Michel de Montaigne*

11

THE ETERNAL QUEST

WHEN MAN EMERGED FROM SAVAGERY HE DID NOT CEASE
from pondering on the mysteries of life and death. He thought
about them on a higher level and his thinking became refined
and systematized. During the long centuries of his upward
struggle he developed philosophy and theology and set aside
as an honored caste his philosophers and theologians. The
tribal medicine man was slowly replaced by the priest, the
teacher, the physician. The old conception of the soul as the
shadow, or as the "little animal inside the big animal, the little
man inside the big man," which dwelt in the hair or the brain
or the heart or the totem, gave way to a more complex and
dignified conception in which the soul was formless. No
longer were weapons, food, and wives buried with the warriors; it was recognized that these were "of the earth, earthy"
and could have no part in man's spiritual existence beyond the
grave. The true significance of life (and therefore of death)
was within, not without; it was to be found in the world of
spirit, not the world of matter. The heart and mind of man
were seen to be the sources of knowledge about God and the
soul.

It is difficult to set a date in human history when this slow
transition from an outer to an inner emphasis was completed,
but we first find it made manifest in recognizable terms in that
incomparable Athenian, Socrates—Socrates, who lived from
469 to 399 B.C., when he was executed by his fellow Athe-
nians on a charge of atheism. His work was continued and
clarified by his great pupil, Plato, and Plato's work in turn was
carried on by his pupil, Aristotle. The thinking of these three
men—Socrates, Plato, and Aristotle—is clearly discernible in

most of what modern theology and philosophy teach about the soul and about immortality, for much of it found its way into Christianity.

The basic, revolutionary idea of Socrates and the thing that distinguished him from the philosophers who had preceded him, was his insistence that the outer world, the material life, is to be interpreted by what is within, by the spirit, or mind. Before Socrates, the external world, the world of matter, had been the standard by which the spiritual life was explained. Socrates reversed the process and taught that the key to an understanding of life lay in spirit, not in matter; in the *self*, not in the cosmos. The great phrase that Jesus used to describe the faith of a Christian, "God is a spirit: and they that worship Him must worship Him in spirit and in truth" (John, 4:24), originated with Socrates and was the center of the philosophy of Socrates, Plato, and Aristotle.

These three Greek philosophers—and particularly Plato—have provided us with the foundation for our modern conception of the soul, and our modern doctrine of immortality. The soul (Plato called it the *reason,* or *Nous*) is a bit of God in man, a spark of the Eternal. As such it cannot die. The material body is its house, or its prison, from which it longs for deliverance. It is this combination—God in man, spirit in body—which is responsible for the incongruities of human experience, for what St. Paul calls the war of the law of the spirit against the law of the flesh.

From all this, Plato deduced that the soul was eternal, and as such knew no beginning or end. Before there was any material world the soul existed as pure spirit. The soul was united with the body in birth, but it was really independent of the body. And the incarnation of the soul in a body was something that (since the soul was eternal and independent) happened not only once but many times, and in many forms. The sage could be reborn as a bird, the warrior as an animal, etc.

This part of Plato's reasoning, of course, was not taken over by Christianity—indeed, was later effectively refuted by his pupil, Aristotle. But reincarnation was very much a part of the serious philosophical and theological thinking of Greece. Socrates defends the doctrine in the *Phaedo.* Empedocles once observed that "I, too, have been a boy, a girl, a bush, a bird, and a scaly fish in the sea." Pythagoras was once moved to pity when he saw some men beating a dog and bade them forbear because the cry of the dog had revealed a friend of his housed in the body of the cur.

While a good deal of the Christian teaching about the soul can be traced back to the Greeks, Greece was not the only place in the world where philosophers were pondering the mysteries of life and death. Long before Plato formulated his doctrine of immortality, the sages of India were working out their systems. At first, reincarnation, or the transmigration of souls, was not a part of Indian philosophy, but very early in history Hinduism turned to this idea, which we have already seen in a simplified form in Plato, and made of it the central doctrine of its whole faith.

Hinduism, however, extended the idea of reincarnation to every form of life and made it a doctrine of unrelieved darkness. The fly you brush away, the insect you crush beneath your foot, even the tiny flea on the fly, may be reincarnations of ancestors of yours, doing penance for sins committed in some previous incarnation. This endless round of birth and rebirth is only broken by withdrawing from the material world and concentrating thought on the Absolute, on God. Life is a penalty, the whole material world is evil and an illusion, and the only salvation comes through self-abnegation and the achievement of a mystical unity with God. Buddhism carried this pessimistic doctrine one step further by teaching that even the idea of oneness with the Absolute was an illusion and that the man who would be delivered from the dreary round of incarnation must overcome even his desire to be one with God.

For both the ancient Greeks and the Hindus, life was a burden to be borne until the soul could break the round of birth and rebirth and unite with God. Personal immortality was not considered desirable or possible. Of all the major world religions and philosophical systems, it remained for Judaism to evolve a doctrine of individual immortality. And it was out of the background of Judaism that the Christian conception of the soul's life after the death of the body developed. In the early Christian Church this conception inherited from Judaism was given overtones of Platonism by the Church's gentile converts, but it remained and still is essentially a flowering from the Hebrew stock—although the Hebrew idea of the soul, in the later stages of its development, was also influenced by the Greeks.

At first, Judaism was not much concerned with life after death. It was this life that was important, and the best that a man could hope for was many years to enjoy it. After it, there was Sheol, and while Sheol was not a place of punishment, there was not much pleasure there. It was more a place of monotony than anything else, and the souls of the dead were pale shades who spent eternity in the feeblest kind of activity. The writer of the Book of Ecclesiastes sums up this early Hebrew pessimism about a future life when he observes that we must do our work with all our might while life lasts, for "there is no work, nor device, nor knowledge, nor wisdom in Sheol, whither we are going." (Ecclesiastes 9:10.)

As long as Israel held to its messianic hope of future prosperity and freedom, this shadowy and inconclusive conception of life after death persisted. The sorrows and trials of the individual in this world were merely reflections of the sorrows and trials of the whole nation, and when the coming of the Messiah ended the nation's troubles, the individual's difficulties would also be over. The messianic hope emphasized the nation and not the individual, and only when the messianic hope weakened did the great teachers of Israel turn their attention to the individual soul. The Exile helped to break the messianic expectation of the nation, and after it we find a new emphasis on the worth of the individual and a new interest in the immortality of the individual soul. The prophet Jeremiah was among the first to express this new insight; in his writings and in the writings of Isaiah we find the emphasis is not on the nation but on the "saving remnant" within the nation. No longer is the national ideal the princely Messiah, but the suffering servant who out of pity and compassion willingly bears the iniquities of all. Salvation becomes transformed from a social to an individual matter, and Sheol is changed from a monotonous habitat of vague souls to a place much like the Christian heaven, where the individual soul may enjoy communion with God. Something very like the Christian resurrection idea then appears in Israel, and the prophet Isaiah cries out:

> Awake and sing, ye that dwell in the dust:
> Thy dead shall live; my dead bodies shall arise.
> (Isaiah 26:19)

With the transformation of Sheol from a shadowy spiritual underworld to a place of ethical judgment where the good soul might commune with God, the foundation was laid for the Christian faith in immortality. And Christianity, with its emphasis on the love and mercy of God, gave to the idea of immortality which men had held since the days of savagery its loftiest and sweetest expression.

A belief in the soul's life after the death of the body is the central doctrine of Christianity. The ancient Hebrews had affirmed such a faith and so had the Greeks. But Jesus of Nazareth not only taught a doctrine of immortality, He lived it and proved it by His return to life after the death on the Cross.

Biblical scholars and others may quibble over what actually happened on the first Easter morning. Did Jesus return in a physical body or a spiritual body? It is not clear. He was recognizable, and Thomas could feel the wound in His side. But He was no longer subject to the laws of matter and could pass instantly through walls from one room to another. St. Paul insisted that what was buried as a physical body was raised as a spiritual body.

It really doesn't matter. What does matter is that Jesus demonstrated the fact that death is not final.

And without this demonstration, there would probably have been no Christian Church. The disciples were dispirited and disheartened; the Messiah in whom they had put their trust had been executed like a common criminal and the authorities were congratulating themselves that an incipient religious revolution had been put down. It was only after Emmaus and the appearance of the Risen Christ in the upper room that the disciples found the courage to "go to the uttermost parts of the earth . . . and preach the gospel to all nations." The Christian Church is founded squarely on the doctrine of the immortality of the individual soul—a personal immortality in which the soul enjoys communion with God while still retaining all the recognizable attributes of personality; an ethical immortality which is based on righteous living here on earth.

To Hindus and, to a lesser extent, to the Greeks, immortality was not especially a happy thing. To the Hindus, the soul was burdened by the load of life in any incarnation. The Greeks admitted that the next incarnation might be either better or worse than this one, but for them, too, life was a prison. But to the Christian, life was a challenge because it was a preparation for eternity, and eternity itself was joyous because in it one would know God and be reunited with all one's earth-friends.

In the early Church this faith in immortality was so strong that the Church fathers had to pass stern laws against the seeking of martyrdom. And the catacombs, or secret burial places of Christians, were not dark and forbidding crypts but places of light, flowers, and even music.

The Christian attitude toward life after death was expressed in all its sweetness and joyousness by Bernard of Cluny, a twelfth century monk, in his *Hora Novissima*. For him, heaven is "Jerusalem the Golden," blessed with milk and honey:

> The Home of fadeless splendor,
>   Of flowers that fear no thorn,
> Where they shall dwell as children,
>   Who here as exiles mourn.
> Midst power that knows no limit,
>   And wisdom free from bound,
> The Beatific Vision
>   Shall glad the saints around:
> The peace of all the faithful,
>   The calm of all the blest,
> Inviolate, unvaried,
>   Divinest, sweetest, best.
> Yes, peace! for war is needless,—
>   Yes, calm! for storm is past,—
> And goal from finished labor,
>   And anchorage at last.*

Suffice it to say that it is in Christianity, with its Hebrew base and Platonic overtones, that we find the fullest, strongest, and most poignant expression of man's intuitive longing for a life beyond the grave.

Not only has immortality been a doctrine of the Christian Church, it has also been a postulate or a hypothesis of the greatest of Western philosophers—not all of them Christians. Plato held that life was a meditation or practicing of death. To Montaigne, death was the beginning of another life and to philosophize was to learn to die. For Immanuel Kant, man's destination was not restricted to the conditions and limits of this life but reached into the infinite. To Henri Bergson, the hypothesis that the soul survives the death of the body appeared "natural and probable." To Pascal, man was a blade of grass, but a blade of grass that could *think*, and therefore something more than the whole material universe. Plotinus thought of death as "the flight of the alone to the alone." The Chinese philosopher Chuang Tsu likened the man who dreads to die to a child who has lost the way home. Spinoza taught that "the soul tends to persist in its being with indefinite dura-

---

* *Seven Great Hymns of the Medieval Church* [New York: A. D. F. Randolph Co., 1868].

tion and is aware of its persistency." Miguel de Unamuno, in his *Tragic Sense of Life,* speaks of "another world, in which destiny is overcome and liberty is law." To Tom Paine it appeared "more probable . . . that I shall continue to exist hereafter than that I should have had existence." And Jean-Jacques Rousseau, the arch-skeptic, could write to his friend, Voltaire: "I have too much suffered in this life not to expect another one. All the subtleties of metaphysics will not make me doubt for a minute the immortality of the soul and a beneficent Providence. I know it, I believe it, I wish it, I hope it, and I will uphold it to my last breath."

One great religious philosopher who was also a great scientist not only affirmed a belief in immortality but actually claimed to have visited heaven and conversed with the souls of the departed. This was no crackpot, but a man of such stature and standing in the academic world that Immanuel Kant wrote a book about him—Emanuel Swedenborg.

Swedenborg's life, according to the Cambridge scholar F. W. H. Myers, was "the strangest ever lived by mortal man." His position in philosophy was such that even today he is known as the Northern Plato. He was born in 1688 in Sweden and was the son of a Lutheran bishop. As a scientist, he was far ahead of his time; writing in 1734 he predicted an atomic theory, developed a theory of the solar origin of the earth, the undulatory theory of light, the nebular hypothesis and many other principles which were later proved valid. The publication of his *Regnum Animale* caused him to be compared favorably with Aristotle. Myers tells us that "It was to Swedenborg first that the unseen world appeared before all things as a realm of law, a region not of mere emotional vagueness and stagnancy of adoration, but of definite progress, according to the laws of cause and effect, resulting from structural laws of spiritual existence and intercourse."

With the same calm rationality with which he discussed tides, geological formations, and the principles of physics, Swedenborg talked about the spiritual world. He was clairvoyant and could predict coming events with regularity and precision. In September 1759, while visiting in Gothenberg, he described for his hosts a fire which had just broken out in Stockholm, three hundred miles away! He was able to describe the progress of the fire in detail just as though he were present, and later his description was verified in published reports of the fire and the accounts of eyewitnesses. In his *Heavenly Arcana,* Swedenborg describes in the same calm, factual way his "journeys" to heaven and his conversations with angels and friends who had passed on.

Swedenborg, of course, was unique. Did he actually see what he says he saw? It is hard to say. But he was no fool, and nobody ever alleged that he was. His fellow scientists, unable to explain Swedenborg or to cope with the questions that his experiences raised, simply ignored him. But today the psychologists, at any rate, are taking Swedenborg seriously.*

Swedenborg was the forerunner of the considerable number of scientists already discussed here who departed from the prevailing materialism of modern science to exhibit a concern for the spiritual world and its phenomena.

The ignorant man, the savage, felt intuitively that he was immortal. The learned man, the philosopher, reasons that he is immortal because only thus does life make sense. The Christian theologian believes in immortality because Jesus of Nazareth taught it and proved it, and because without it the goodness and justice of God can be called into question. Injustice, he points out, is so obvious in this world that if there is not another world in which redress is possible, God cannot be either just or moral; either that or God is not good, in which case the true divine arbiter is Satan.

So men at all levels of cultural development from savagery to modern times have believed in life after death. They have *felt* that it was so, they have *reasoned* that it ought to be so, they have had *faith* that it was so.

But does that *make* it so?

No. It does not make it so because *science* has not said it was so. And it is *science,* not philosophy or theology or art or literature or metaphysics, that is the basic authority of our day. Why does not science join with philosophy and religion in affirming it? Because science has to have proof, demonstration. Until science says that immortality is a fact, the mass of mankind will wish it to be so and feel that it is so, but will not *know* with that knowledge that lifts the heart. The indications are favorable. Today science through its "advance guard" in psychology is re-examining its whole materialistic position and is providing us with some amazing evidence on this ancient question of survival.

The day that mankind *knows* that it is truly free from what St. Paul called "the law of sin and death" will be the greatest

---

*For a good modern biography of Swedenborg, see Signe Toksvig, *Emanuel Swedenborg* [New Haven: Yale University Press, 1948].

day in the history of the human race. That knowledge will un-
lock all the creative and artistic energies of man and result in
a cultural and spiritual flowering such as the earth has not
known since the early days of Christianity.

How near is that day? Very near indeed.

So let the soul that is not unworthy of that vision contemplate the Great Soul; freed from deceit and every witchery, and collected into calm. Calmed be the body for her in that hour, and the tumult of the flesh; ay, all that is about her, calm; calm be the earth, the sea, the air, and let Heaven itself be still. Then let her feel how into that silent Heaven the the Great Soul floweth in. . . . And so may man's soul be sure of Vision, when suddenly she is filled with light; for this light is from Him and is He; and then surely shall one know His presence when, like a god of old time, He entered into the house of one that calleth Him, and maketh it full of light.

—Plotinus

12

MAN *IS* IMMORTAL

IN THESE PAGES SO FAR WE HAVE EXAMINED CAREFULLY all the evidence we can bring together on Job's question: "If a man die, shall he live again?" We have seen how the natural belief in immortality, the intuitive faith of the savage, flowered into the sweet and moving Judeo-Christian idea of a final resurrection and reunion in heaven. We have looked at the phenomena that convinced the unofficial scientific researchers in the American and British Societies for Psychical Research of the fact of immortality—the phantasms, the evidence from mediumship, the cross-correspondences, the automatic speech and writing, the book tests. We have traced the development of the new science of parapsychology and have seen how it has established experimentally the existence of a spiritual component, or soul, in man; a human faculty that is not limited by space or time. We have studied precognitive dreams and theories of Time that seem to indicate that our conception of it as divided into past, present, and future may not correspond to reality. We have become cognizant of the experience of those who, like Emanuel Swedenborg, claim to have transcended space and time while still in this life.

We have seen, too, how science has become steadily less and less materialistic in its evaluation of life and how the idea of God, once considered intolerable and even ridiculous by science, is now increasingly accepted as the most probable hypothesis for the existence of the cosmos and its life. And finally, in the newest branch of science, parapsychology, we have heard the most modern, the most advanced of the nuclear psychologists affirming, on the basis of laboratory experiment and clinical demonstration, that "the soul theory has been confirmed," and that "we can now conceive of the idea of God as a rational hypothesis." And finally we have seen that the inevitable corollary of the idea of God is the idea of the immortality of the individual soul.

Now "science," of course, is a word that means different things to different people. It means one thing to the so-called "Christian Scientist," and quite another thing to the biochemist. It covers a multitude of strange bedfellows ranging from the psychoanalyst and his couch to the airplane designer with his blueprints. It includes the geometrician and his precise theorems and the Einsteinian physicist with his abstract hypotheses. It is a blanket term, just as "religion" is. When we say that "religion says" we do not necessarily mean that Hinduism, Shintoism, Jainism, and Judaism all say the same thing, because obviously they do not. When we say "the law says," we do not mean that American, Russian, and Chinese law all agree on a proposition, or even that the laws of New York, Illinois, and California agree. What we mean is that a particular religion or a particular legal code affirms a certain proposition at a certain time.

So it is with science. All scientists, of course, do not believe in God or in immortality (but the best of them, I think, do). Moreover, no one is empowered to speak for all of science, just as no one is empowered to speak for all of religion or all of law. So when I say that "science says" I do not mean that any scientific *nihil obstat* has now been stamped on the idea of God or immortality. Indeed, there is still a great deal of hostility in the heterogeneous family of science to those ideas. But I *do* mean that an established and respected branch of science which is particularly concerned with this area of human thought and experience has now established both God and the human soul as *working hypotheses,* and has demonstrated the validity of these hypotheses with utmost scientific rigor in its laboratories.

Moreover, science differs from religion and law in that it is not a body of codified truth to which reference may be made (as Christians may refer to the Bible or lawyers to the Constitution) but a *method.* This method is deduction based on observation and experiment under laboratory conditions. Science in the broadest sense is that which studies phenomena according to the scientific method. All the phenomena studied in this book have been subjected to the scientific method by trained scientists. Therefore, it is correct to introduce findings arrived at by scientists via the scientific method by announcing that "science says." And it is in that sense that we affirm here that science (not all of science, nor all scientists) now says that man *is immortal*.

And if some wayward biochemist or nuclear physicist or geologist contradicts us and says that *he* cannot subscribe to the idea of a spiritual component in life and that his branch of science cannot subscribe to any such hypothesis, we can simply say: No, but parapsychology does and the parapsychologists do and this is their special field, not yours. Just as we would accept a Lutheran bishop as a better spokesman on Lutheran Church polity than an Anglican bishop, or a civil law expert as a better spokesman on the civil code than a counselor whose specialty was criminal law, so we must accept the parapsychologist as a better spokesman on matters dealing with the psyche, or soul, than the nuclear physicist whose specialty is the atom, or the geologist whose specialty is the substratum.

What *does* parapsychology say? It says that the idea of God is now a rational hypothesis, and that the soul-theory has been confirmed. Moreover, it says that this soul, or spiritual component in the individual, is not subject to the limitations of space-time, and that the logical inference may thereby be drawn that it survives that enforcement of space-time limitation which we call death. It does not, of course, say at this point just what it is that survives, or how much of it may be presumed to survive, nor for how long, nor under what limitations. Those questions remain for the parapsychological research that still goes forward. And in this research, parapsychology can now count on the cooperation of scientists from all the related fields, from mathematics to cultural anthropology.*

Perhaps the chief significance of the findings of parapsychology is their confirmation of the soul-theory, the existence in life of a real, non-material component. Next to that in significance is the new light the recent findings throw on the

*See "The Question of Spirit Survival," *Journal of the American Society for Psychical Research* [New York], Vol. XLII, No. 2 [April, 1949].

older work of the psychical researchers—the studies of phantasms, the hallucinations, the veridical dreams, the mediumships; the cross-correspondences, the automatisms, the book tests. In the light of parapsychology, all these take on an evidential character that they did not possess before. And finally, parapsychology opens up a new frontier for scientific research—the mind frontier. On this new frontier the most vital and meaningful pioneering the human race has ever known may now go forward. Thus the political, religious, and economic revolutions that have so changed life in the modern period now give way to the psychological revolution. When that revolution is done with us the face of life will be so transformed as to be unrecognizable to mid-twentieth-century man.

If immortality, what kind of immortality? We do not know. However, Professor Hornell Hart of Duke University, in the Garvin Lecture which he delivered at Lancaster, Pennsylvania in 1943, draws some conclusions on the basis of all the available evidence from psychical research. According to reports allegedly received from the spirit-world through mediums, and from statements made by people who claim to have made excursions into the abode of the dead through near-death, dreams, or dissociation, they find themselves, at or near the point of death, *outside* of their physical bodies but unable to get back into them. They say that they were able to see their old surroundings, possessions, and friends, but could not make themselves seen, felt, or heard. Just before death they began to be aware of friends or loved ones who had died previously, and were able to see, touch, and converse with them. There is a tendency on the part of the newly dead to hang around their old haunts on earth for a while, still trying to experience the old bodily gratifications. Sometimes the newly dead are successful in taking partial possession of the living and thus enjoying the delights of the flesh vicariously. Usually, however, they are taken in hand by old friends or relatives or by other ministering spirits and introduced gradually to a new kind of life—a life in which they are surrounded by objects which they can see and touch. Among these are landscapes, buildings, furniture, books, plants, people, and even animals. These *look* at first exactly like their counterparts on earth, and particularly like the surroundings in a vivid dream. But they are really different, being molded by the thoughts, desires, and purposes of the deceased individual. In this afterworld, it is possible to travel by a mere act of will and to create by intense imagination, particularly collective imagination.

There are many different regions in this afterworld, some where people are happy and some where they are unhappy. The various regions have different interests, occupations, and activities and the individual after death tends to gravitate into regions where he associates with people who are like himself. Here his environment is created jointly out of the collective memories, attitudes, and desires of those who are spiritually in tune with him. If he is sensual and selfish he finds himself in the kind of an environment that sensual and selfish people would subconsciously create in their interactions with one another, and he has to remain in this state until he has gained enough insight to move on to a higher level of thought and activity. On the other hand, if he is altruistic and noble he lives in the kind of an environment that altruistic and noble individuals would create by the interactions of their personalities, and he progresses from that higher level.*

Now, this is admittedly a rather fanciful picture of the afterlife, and cannot claim any sort of a scientific sanction. I offer it here merely as a matter of interest; the reader will have to evaluate it for what he thinks it is worth in the light of all that has gone before in this book.

Sometimes very practical information allegedly comes from the "other side." A good illustration of such information is the Case of the Dutch Ambassador's Lost Receipt, which Immanuel Kant reports in his book on Swedenborg, *Dreams of a Spirit-Seer* (London: S. Sonnenschein & Co. Ltd., 1900), pp. 157-158:

Madame Herteville (Marteville), the widow of the Dutch Ambassador in Stockholm, some time after the death of her husband, was called upon by Croon, a goldsmith, to pay for a silver service which her husband had purchased from him. The widow was convinced that her late husband had been much too precise and orderly not to have paid this debt, yet she was unable to find the receipt. In her sorrow, and because the amount was considerable, she requested Mr. Swedenborg to call at her house. After apologizing to him for troubling him, she said that if, as all people said, he possessed the extraordinary gift of conversing with the souls of

*Professor Hornell Hart is a sociologist. He was in charge of measuring changes in social attitudes for President Herbert Hoover's Committee on Social Trends. His lecture is contained in the book *Man's Destiny in Eternity* [Boston: Beacon Press, 1949].

the departed, he would perhaps have the kindness to ask her husband how it was about the silver service. Swedenborg did not at all object to comply with her request. Three days afterward the said lady had company at her house for coffee. Swedenborg called and in his cool way informed her that he had conversed with her husband. The debt had been paid several months before his decease, and the receipt was in a bureau in the room upstairs. The lady replied that the bureau had been quite cleared out, and that the receipt was not found among all the papers. Swedenborg said that her husband had described to him, how after pulling out the left-hand drawer a board would appear, which required to be drawn out, when a secret compartment would be disclosed, containing his private Dutch correspondence, as well as the receipt. Upon hearing this description the whole company arose and accompanied the lady into the room upstairs. The bureau was opened; they did as they were directed; the compartment was found, of which no one had ever known before; and to the great astonishment of all, the papers were discovered there, in accordance with his description.

It does, however, raise one question with which we may well concern ourselves for a moment. It shows us objects in the next world which are very like the material objects we know in this one, and we know not only from this but from other and less imaginative evidence that the spiritual body seems to be very much like the material body. It apparently retains the physical characteristics of the earth-life, and even in some cases wears clothes. When Harry Price touched "Rosalie," he discovered that this "spirit" had the kind of tangible body that one might expect a normal child of her age to have. And Christians and Jews have always held "the resurrection of the body" as a tenet of faith, although much of the later New Testament teaching has insisted on a spiritual interpretation of the resurrection. Most liberal Christians and Jews no longer believe in a resurrection of the physical body, even though they still give lip-service to the creeds that affirm it. And on the face of it, a physical resurrection seems an absurdity.

Perhaps, and perhaps not.

In dreams, we are all aware of physical objects that, while we are dreaming, have all the tangibility and color of their counterparts that we know in the waking state. We observe minute details. We experience heat and cold. We fall down very real stairs and sustain very real blows. Our emotions are genuine. The people we meet in dreams are just as real (while we are dreaming) as the people we know when we are awake, and they affect us in much the same way. Human beings whom we meet in dreams do not differ much, if at all, from the human beings we meet in everyday life. And this dream-life is probably the nearest thing we have to our actual life beyond the grave, for in dreams the psyche, or mind, is free from time and space limitation, just as the soul must be in the afterworld. Indeed, so real and "alive" can our dreams be that some authors—notably Kipling in *Brushwood Boy* and George du Maurier in *Peter Ibbetson*—have their lovers sharing rendezvous in dreams. This is not as fanciful as it sounds—there are numerous cases on record in which people have reported actual *shared* dreams, in which two or more people meet, observe their common surroundings, talk, and engage in various activities which all concerned remember on awaking. The dream-world, at any rate, is a world very much like the waking one.

Now the spiritual component in man that has been demonstrated in the laboratories of parapsychology—his soul—is certainly non-material. It cannot be corrupted or disintegrated, cannot lose its unity or its internal energy. It cannot "die" as the body dies. The French Catholic philosopher Jacques Maritain says of it:

Each of us is inhabited. With what wonderful respect we would look upon every human being, if we thought of that invisible Psyche who dwells within him and who causes him to be what he is, and who will endure longer than the world, endure always, after these poor bones are reduced to dust! How can our eyes contemplate any human person without seeking anxiously after the eternal mystery which is living in him? The first Christians kissed the breasts of their children with awe and veneration, thinking of that eternal presence within them. They had some idea, some awareness, less fickle than ours, of the immortality of the human soul.*

But, says Maritain, precious as that psyche, that soul, is, it is not a *person*. We are concerned here with the immortality of the person, the essence of the individual, and that personality seems to be inseparable from the physical form we know here on earth. A complete "person" is *both* body and soul. Hence, the immortality for which we yearn is an immortality not of the soul alone but of the whole person.

*"The Immortality of Man."

Here, says Maritain, is where the Hindu conception of the afterlife differs from the Judeo-Christian. In the former, the soul surrenders the immortality of the person. It lives after the dissolution of the person by death by *metempsychosis,* or transmigration. Thus the same soul has a succession of personalities, a succession of lives, and these personalities and lives are gone forever once the soul leaves them.

The Judeo-Christian conception, on the other hand, is a conception, a philosophy, of the Final End—that is, in the Final End the *Person* is restored and then lives as a Person in eternity without further sundering. Thus the doctrine of the "resurrection" or restoration of the "body." It is the Person that is resurrected and restored, through the grace of God, who is Himself personal. How is this possible? Because "grace perfects Nature," says Maritain.

This argument, too, cannot have scientific sanction. But we are speculating here, and in our speculation on personal immortality, Maritain's argument, like Hornell Hart's, deserves our attention.

In conclusion it may well be asked: what do you personally believe about immortality? How much of all this evidence, experiment, and speculation do *you* accept?

For a long, long time, I did not accept any of it. My college and graduate school period was the "jazz age," the fabulous twenties and early thirties, when boom was followed by bust and the cult of Mencken and F. Scott Fitzgerald gave way to the frenzies of Marx and the proletarian novel. It was a time in which God was only "a cretin's nightmare dream" and religion "the opiate of the people." I swallowed Mencken and washed him down with copious draughts of *Das Kapital* and Freud. To me—to all of us in those days—things *were* what they seemed. Even in theological seminary the quality of the dandelion wine that future Methodist bishops were vinting in their dormitory bathtubs seemed much more important than the immortality of the soul, or lack of same.

As a matter of fact, all through college, seminary, graduate school, and the early years in social work and the ministry, I just did not think about the matter. At funerals I repeated the customary phrases and was able to assert a confidence in their validity that assuaged many a bereaved spirit. But I refused to concern myself with the idea of immortality, and insofar as I thought about it all, I entertained large doubts that any such thing was possible or even desirable. I do not think my attitude differed greatly from that of the other young, liberal Protestant clergymen of my age. We were too preoccupied with the problems of this world to concern ourselves with the next, if there was a next.

I think it was World War II in general, and the explosion of the first atomic bomb over Hiroshima in particular, that made me realize the basic emptiness of a philosophy of life that bypassed consideration of immortality. With the advent of the atomic bomb, life on earth had become too perilous, too tentative, to be lived without reference to another life; the injustices and defeats of the spirit of man in this temporal existence had become too monstrous to be borne, unless it was posible to redeem them somewhere beyond time. Time, as Aldous Huxley points out in *Times Must Have a Stop*, is meaningless except as a point of reference in eternity. It was in this spirit that I was introduced for the first time to the writings of Dr. J. B. Rhine and began to acquire an interest in parapsychology. Dr. Rhine had read an article of mine in *The American Mercury*, and he wrote me about it. The result of the extended correspondence that then ensued was an avid reading of all of the published works of Dr. Rhine, a series of visits to the Parapsychology Laboratory at Duke University, and a participation in the experiments that were being conducted there. Out of all this came two books, *Religion and the New Psychology*, and *The Psychic Source-Book*, which Eileen Garrett of *Tomorrow* magazine induced me to edit. The research required for all this familiarized me with the extensive literature of the American and British Societies for Psychical Research and the works of men like F. W. H. Myers, William McDougall, Harry Price, Carl Jung, and many other psychical researchers and psychologists. The result has been an abiding interest in this field and a firm faith that immortality is a fact.

I came to this conclusion, therefore, from the scientific rather than from the psychical side. My interest in mediumship, cross-correspondences, phantasms, poltergeists, etc. *followed*, it did not precede, my own study. I looked at the phenomena of psychical research in the light of my studies in parapsychology—and as a result discarded as nonsense about nine-tenths of what I found in the former. But I knew that the one-tenth that was *not* nonsense was world-shaking in its implications.

What do I believe? That nothing is lost; that values are eternal; that there is a Designer who is Good, and a soul that is immortal; that Eternity is a real and pleasant place; that we live in it now and that we shall live in it forever as the same persons that we are today; that the opportunity for growth and development does not end with death. I believe that after the experience we call death I will see and know—yes, and love—those who have preceded me in that experience: my father and mother, the little cousin who died in infancy, the dear grandparents, the classmates lost on Iwo Jima and at Omaha Beach. I think I have looked objectively at all the evidence and discarded that which was in the least suspect. I think I have listened to all the arguments both pro and con and heard all the jokes and suffered all the little indignities incidental to serious research in this field. And after all this, with whatever authority may have accrued to me or "come off" on me as a result of my association, personally and through the printed word, with men and women whose intelligence and reputation are far beyond mine, I am constrained to say: man is immortal.

*I shall light a candle of understanding
in thine heart, which shall not be put out.*
—*2 Esdras XIV, 25*

13

IN THE LIGHT
OF ETERNITY

WE HAVE TAKEN OUR LONG LONG LOOK AT JOB'S QUES-
tion: "If a man die, shall he live again?" We have decided that
the answer is "Yes," that man is immortal, that we live not in
time, but in eternity.

This knowledge is the "candle of understanding" that God
has placed in our hearts. Does it make a difference, this light?
Does it illumine the darkness? Does it assuage the bereaved
spirit?

The assurance that man is immortal and that death does not
have dominion over him makes all the difference in the world
in our relations with God and our cosmic environment, with
our fellow men, and with ourselves.

First, with God and nature. Without the light from this candle of understanding it is hard for us to love God and the
world which surrounds us. Truly, without immortality man is
"born to trouble as the sparks fly upward"; all that he loves
and labors for lies beneath the Damocleian sword of death; all
his dearest relationships are sundered; all his high purposes
and plans brought to naught. In all that he does he is frus-
trated; in all that he is he is incomplete; all that he loves he
loses. And nature, whose inexorable processes bring him to
this end in time, is his foe, "red of fang and claw." Can man
glorify the God who sets the mark of doom upon him? Can he
feel at home in a world the dimensions of which are, finally,
the 6 by 3 of the grave?

No. But in the light of this candle of understanding man
sees himself, in truth, as a child of God; he sees the Creator as
the source and center of love, "in whom is no variableness nor
shadow of turning"; he opens his eyes on a world in which the

162

processes of nature are but part of a grand and purposive plan. He can be at home in such a world; he can know the joy of a St. Francis in fellowship with all who share it with him. Its vistas and sunsets and autumns, its myriad forms of life, its tender, innocent creatures—these things touch him and claim him and fill him with intimations of immortality.

It is this candle of understanding that provides us with light on our eternal pilgrimage to find and know God. And this pilgrimage is the chief end of life. In *Of Time and the River*, Thomas Wolfe says of it:

> Where shall the weary rest? When shall the lonely of heart come home? What doors are open for the wanderer? And which of us shall find his father, know his face, and in what place and in what time and in what land? Where? Where the weary of heart can abide forever, where the weary of wandering can find peace, where the tumult, the fever, and the fret shall be forever stilled?

And Wolfe ends his magnificent essay on human loneliness:

> Immortal love, alone and aching in the wilderness, we cried to you; you were not absent from our loneliness.*

That father, whose footprints we follow through the world forever, and whose face we have never seen, can be viewed at last only in the light that comes from that candle of understanding which He Himself has placed in our hearts for that very purpose. "Little we see in Nature that is ours" without it, but with it we see the Creator in His handiwork, we are aware that every tree, every bush, is aflame with God. In that light, we can watch the flight of the wild geese southward in the fall and know with the poet William Cullen Bryant that:

> He who, from zone to zone,
> Guides through the boundless skies thy certain
>   flight:
> In the long way that I must tread alone,
> Will lead my steps aright.†

The light of immortality illumines the world in which we live and leads us to God.

---

*Thomas Wolfe, *The Face of a Nation* [New York: Charles Scribner's Sons, 1939].
†"To a Waterfowl," in *Complete Poems of William Cullen Bryant* [New York: Frederick A. Stokes], p. 26.

Second, in our relations with our fellow men, how can we hate, how can we exploit, how can we kill, the brothers who share with us the treasure of immortality? Time-obsession is the root of much of the evil in our world; the time-obsessed religious faiths are the persecuting, proselytizing ones. Intolerance has its foundation in time-obsession. So does greed. We covet, we hoard, because we are running a terrible race with time; there is so little time, we think, to find and enjoy the good things of life. So to get them (and often we do not even know what they are) we scratch and bite and fight and cheat.

We treat men in accordance with what we think they are. When we think of some races and groups as "inferior" we discriminate against them, we exploit them, we kill them, with little compunction. When we do not see God in men we treat them like the devil—literally. And so without God, and that belief in immortality which is the concomitant of God, we act like beasts in a jungle; survival for as long as possible is our only law.

But light that candle of understanding and the jungle turns into a garden; the law of survival is nullified because there is no such thing as non-survival; the law of competition is negated because we have all of eternity to find and enjoy the good life.

The East can teach us here. There is no time-obsession in the religions of the Orient. This passivity of the East is alien to us; we do not understand it. But we can learn from it. In Jean Renoir's beautiful and moving film of India, *The River*, there is a scene where the crippled American soldier, raving against the fate that has overtaken him, asks the Hindu girl what he can do to make life worthwhile. She answers him in one word that sums up all the difference between East and West: "Consent."

Consent? Yes, consent to circumstance, for circumstance is passing and temporal, but life is eternal. Consent to life, to God, to the processes that sometimes bring us happiness and sometimes unhappiness, sometimes health and sometimes sickness, but that inevitably pass and, whether we like them or not, advance us a little farther on that pilgrimage which is the chief end of our earthly existence. Consent, in the spirit of Job, who cried out in the midst of his sore affliction: "Though he slay me, yet will I love Him!"

At the western end of the Midway at the University of Chicago stands Lorado Taft's majestic sculpture group called

"The Fountain of Time." The idea for it is based on Austin Dobson's couplet:

Time goes, you say? Ah, no,
Alas, time stays. We go.

In this great work one sees the mighty, craglike figure of Time, face shrouded, leaning upon a staff and watching with inscrutable gaze the endless march of humanity. Past the silent, mantled figure hurries an endless procession of men, women, and children, "ever impelled by the winds of Destiny in the inexorable lock-step of the ages." Theirs is the fateful, forward movement which has not ceased since time began. "But," says Lorado Taft, "in that crowded concourse how few detach themselves from the grayness of the dusky caravan, how few there are who even lift their heads. Here an overtaxed body falls—and a place is vacant for a moment; there a strong man turns to the shrouded reviewer and with lifted arms utters the cry of the old-time gladiators: 'Hail, Caesar, we who go to our death salute thee'—and presses forward."[*]

The feeling produced by this great piece of sculpture is one of unutterable sadness. From dark to dark we go, the hurrying figures seem to be saying, with only a little light in between. The mood induced in that of Ecclesiastes—"Vanity of vanities . . . all is vanity."

And without the light of immortality, all is indeed vanity. Our brother men are but fellow pilgrims on an endless journey to nothingness. If they fall we need not help them up, for soon we, too, shall fall, and between their fall and ours is but a moment of time. If they inconvenience us they can be thrust aside (if we are stronger than they are!). When we think of other men, and of ourselves, as mere temporary victims of the disease of consciousness, love and compassion are a waste of time and a sign of weakness.

But light the candle of understanding, and the face of Time is revealed as smiling. It is our friend, not our foe. We move past it, not toward extinction, but toward glad reunions and new insights and higher levels of aspiration and life. And those who journey with us are not foes, not competitors, but friends and brothers who like ourselves bear upon their foreheads the caste-mark of divinity. In the light of immortality differences fade away, wars cease, exploitation and hatred and

[*]Ada B. Taft, *Lorado Taft, Sculptor and Citizen* [Greensboro, N. C., Published by Mary Taft Smith, 1946], p. 36.

intolerance are no more. For these are the things of time, and of death—and "death no longer hath dominion over us." With John Donne we can say:

> Death, be not proud, though some have called thee
> Mighty and dreadful, for thou are not so;
> For those whom you think'st thou dost overthrow
> Die not, poor Death, nor yet canst thou kill me.*

Yes, the light of immortality illumines the dark face of Time and unites us with our fellow pilgrims.

Finally, the assurance of eternal life calms our troubled minds and enables us better to know and understand ourselves. "What is man that thou art mindful of him?" cries the Psalmist. But in the light of the candle of understanding we can answer with St. Augustine: "Thou hast made us for Thyself, and our hearts are restless until they rest in Thee."

Men are groping from peace of mind today as never before, but we cannot have much peace of mind until we know what we are. As long as we consider ourselves mere accidental conglomerations of atoms, chromosomes, and what not, doomed as casually to disintegration as we were to integration, then peace of mind must perforce elude us.

For, in truth, we cannot make peace with death or with the idea of death. Consciousness cannot tolerate the idea of its dissolution. The mind burdened consciously or subconsciously with the fear of doom, of ceasing-to-be, cannot work at its highest efficiency, cannot be really healthy, cannot find the peace it seeks. We become what our fathers used to call "whole" men and women only when life makes sense to us, when it adds up. Perhaps we should say: only if it adds up to *something*. If the sum of life's addition is zero then the cosmic problem involved is not worth solving.

In Arthur Miller's play *Death of a Salesman,* there is a very poignant scene at the grave of the salesman, where his wife cries out against the fate that has brought her husband to penury and suicide. "A man can't come into the world with nothing and then go out with nothing!" she says. "A man has to *add up* to something!"

Yes, if life is to be meaningful, if it is to bring us peace of mind and make us whole, it has to add up to something. And only the assurance of ongoing consciousness, of new opportunities, of a chance to redress injustice, of a reunion with loved ones, makes it add up. When the candle of understand-

*Sonnet, "Death."

ing is lit in our hearts, the dark places of the mind are filled with light, fears and neuroses flee, and a unifying and healing sense of peace descends upon us. It is only then that we know that life, love, and God are good; only then that we are made whole—"one, as the Father is one"—only then that we know the meaning of St. Paul's words: "For I am persuaded, that neither death, nor life, nor angels, nor principalities, nor powers, nor things present, nor things to come, nor height, nor depth, nor any other creature, shall be able to separate us from the love of God." (Romans 8:38-39)

The light of immortality fills the inner recesses of being, heals the troubled mind and body, and brings to us a peace that passes all understanding.

This, then, is what the light of the candle of understanding shows us. This is what a belief in immortality does for us.

If I could reduce eternity to a blueprint and chart the streets of heaven I would gladly do so. If I could draw a picture of the soul and say, "This is it, this is the part of man that lives forever," I would be happy to do it. I am sure there is an eternity and a soul to inhabit it and an ongoing consciousness to preserve forever the loves and ties of earth. I am sure that all that I have loved awaits me and that nothing is lost. This book has been a documentation of that faith. What Santayana called "the soul's invincible surmise" is more than a surmise for me; it is a demonstrated truth.

But much, perhaps most, of life is a mystery and must remain so, at least for a while. I remember back in my college days hearing an old philosophy professor say again and again that God only reveals Himself and His ways to us to the degree that we can understand and use the revelation. Science is pushing aside the curtains that shield the infinite from mortal gaze, but slowly, and perhaps that is all for the best. Someday we shall know. We do not have specific blueprints now, but we do have the master plan, the cosmic conception. That will do us for a long time to come. I know I am going home someday, to where love and God are, and whether "home" is up or down or in, is a matter that does not much concern me.

So for now, turn to that candle of understanding in your heart, and by its light read the message from the Book of Life: "Death is swallowed up in victory."

Then, as you close the Book, gather your loved ones around you, and pray the prayer with which Cardinal Newman began the day:

*O Lord, support us all the day long, until the shadows lengthen and the evening comes, and the busy world is hushed, and the fever of life is over and our work is done. Then in thy mercy grant us a safe lodging, and a holy rest, and peace at the last.**

*From the *Book of Common Prayer.*

Index

INDEX

SIGNET Gothic Novels You Will Enjoy

GRANITE FOLLY *by Caroline Farr*
A headstrong heiress inherits a pirate ancestor's mansion and a legacy of plunder and death.
(#P3242—60¢)

THE INTRUSION *by Elizabeth McCrae*
Her striking resemblance to an Austrian beauty, who had mysteriously disappeared many years before, leads an American tourist to the threshold of romance and violence.
(#P3290—60¢)

THE RIVER AND THE ROSE *by Sandra Abbott*
Trapped in a gloomy Southern mansion and irresistibly drawn toward the handsome, enigmatic master of the house, the heroine of this Gothic novel learns that, because of her uncanny resemblance to a dead woman, her own life is in great danger.
(#P3199—60¢)

VOICES IN THE WIND *by Erika Vaughn Allen*
A writer seeks solitude at a remote mansion in the Ozarks, but instead she finds love and a terrifying legacy of danger and death.
(#P3189—60¢)

THE SHAKING SHADOW *by Elizabeth Stuart*
A young woman is employed as companion to an eccentric dowager who dabbles in seances and entertains nine strangely fascinating relatives torn between greed and terror as they wait for the old woman to die.
(#P3186—60¢)

A SILENT VOICE *by Susan Claudia*
Following a clue in a rare book, the heroine of this Gothic novel journeys to a family castle in France where she becomes caught up in a strange legacy of treason, and involved in an obsessive search for buried treasure.
(#P3181—60¢)

THE SEARCHING SPECTOR *by Susan Claudia*
In a stirring Gothic novel, a young nurse on her first private assignment innocently enters a household of danger and deception.
(#P3155—60¢)

MANSION OF SMILING MASKS *by Daoma Winston*
In this chilling Gothic novel, a woman's love for her husband traps her in a mansion haunted by a long-standing curse.
(#P3136—60¢)

Other SIGNET Books You'll Want to Read